"*Becoming a Dad* is just what I was looking for two years ago as I searched for a book to give my son, a soon to be first-time father . . . Refreshingly free of formulas, *Becoming a Dad* calls husbands and fathers to engage with their hearts, to put their whole selves in, and to travel the mysterious waters of family life with relationship as their highest goal. An important book with application to fathers of all ages and stages."

ANDI ASHWORTH,
author,
Real Love for Real Life

"*Becoming a Dad* is practical and promising, wise and witty. I think new parents need two copies. One for him to take everywhere and one for him to read to her just after he puts the children to bed, runs her bath and rubs her feet. She'll love the book. I promise."

ANGELA THOMAS,
author,
Do You Think I'm Beautiful?

"Excellent—a very important book for dads! What insight!"

LARRY MALONE,
Director, UMMenistries
for General Commission
on United Methodist Men

"Within pages of reading this work, I was longing to raise my sons again. I urge every new father to bless their child by reading this book."

CHIP DODD, Ph.D.,
Executive Director,
Center for Professional Excellence
and author, *The Voice of the Heart*

"If there was any remnant of the notion of a new father as a helpless bystander, Stephen and David have dispelled it for good. With insights both humorous and poignant, they've written a book that should be required reading for all dads."

AL ANDREWS,
director, Porter's Call and co-author, *The Silence of Adam*

"*Becoming a Dad* is an awesome and unique book for men who are preparing for fatherhood! Practical, encouraging, honest, solid, and useful! Don't miss this important resource."

JEFF HELTON,
Congregational Care Pastor,
Fellowship Bible Church, Brentwood, Tennessee

"A masterful, refreshing book that will inspire you to become a different kind of dad."

LINDA BRADY, M.D.,
pediatrician, Old Harding Pediatric Association

"Stephen James and David Thomas give us a heart-warming and up-close look at the privilege of fatherhood. Practical insights mixed with genuinely funny experiences make this book engaging and very helpful."

CARTER CRENSHAW,
Senior Pastor,
West End Community Church, Nashville, Tennessee

"*Becoming a Dad* is a warm, well-lit path toward fatherhood."

MELISSA TREVATHAN AND SISSY GOFF,
authors, *The Back Door to Your Teen's Heart*,
Executive Director and Director of
Child and Adolescent Counseling,
Daystar Counseling Ministries

BECOMING A DAD

A SPIRITUAL, EMOTIONAL AND PRACTICAL GUIDE

STEPHEN JAMES AND DAVID THOMAS

[RELEVANTBOOKS]
WWW.RELEVANTBOOKS.COM

Published by Relevant Books
A division of Relevant Media Group, Inc.

www.relevantbooks.com
www.relevantmediagroup.com

Design: Relevant Solutions
www.relevant-solutions.com
Cover design by Joshua M. Smith, II
Interior design by Joshua M. Smith, II and Jeremy Kennedy

For information or bulk orders:
RELEVANT MEDIA GROUP, INC.
100 SOUTH LAKE DESTINY DRIVE SUITE 200
ORLANDO, FL 32810
PH: (321) 206-8844 FX: (321) 206-3949

International Standard Book Number: 0-9760357-3-1

05 06 07 08 9 8 7 6 5 4 3 2 1

Printed in the United States of America

Feb 28, 2006

Joe,

You have, quite simply, been a comfort and delight to us since your birth.

The idea of your becoming a father doesn't quite seem possible. Seems like only yesterday ~

TO HEATHER AND CONNIE

There is no doubt in our minds that you will be an amazing, and loving, and responsible father.

Being a parent will be the most important job you will ever have and the most meaningful.

i begin each day with a prayer to God for our family and soon there will be a new "little Bird" added to my prayers. My prayer for this newest family member will be that he or she have the loving, kind heart of Mom and Dad.

We offer you, as always, our love and support for this ~ your most important role. The role of Father.

God bless you always,
Mom

CONTENTS

Nothing can prepare you to be a father. Nothing. Not a book, not a long walk in the woods, not a deep conversation with a parenting mentor who will guide you through the labyrinth of complexity related to raising and being raised by your bundle of glory.

You must be asking: Why read a book on becoming a parent when nothing will help? Thanks for asking. I didn't say nothing would help. This book will help so much, you will end up giving a copy to every man you meet who is about to become a father. This is a brilliant, well researched, wonderfully written guide to becoming a good father.

Nothing can prepare you for the wildest ride of your life. First, let me tell you that I am the father of a twenty-four-year-old daughter who is a professional acupuncturist, a nineteen-year-old college student who wants to be a nurse and work with indigent children, and a sixteen-year-old son, who plays bass and sings like Eddie Vedder in a band called Gladys. I am so proud of my children I could weep. I could sometimes collectively ship them off to Siberia. It is a strange, mixed bag to be a father.

I had lunch with a dear friend who is in his twenties who told me his wife is pregnant. There was little joy in his voice. He was in between disbelief and terror. He said bluntly, "We never planned to have children. And then in a matter of a few seconds and an off-the-shelf pregnancy test, I find out I'm going to be a father. I feel like I lost my wife, my life, because an alien is growing in the womb of my wife."

An hour before our time, I was on the phone with an

insurance agent attempting to make a decision about a vehicle my middle child had wrecked. A part of me agreed with my friend, but I wanted to add that alien eventually comes alive outside the womb and is no less strange. It is a strange trip, no question.

Then why have children? Why read a book on fathering? The answer is so simple it nearly makes me cry. When I saw the face of my first daughter after a very traumatic emergency C-section, I never knew such love existed in me. I never knew such love existed anywhere in the universe. It does—in the heart of a parent, in the magnitude of the sea. What you are about to enter is the most magical, life-transforming love relationship of your life. I guarantee you that you will not come out of this relationship unscathed, but the privilege to love and to be loved as a father is by far the most glorious gift one can receive from another human being.

Why not do it better than we might if we didn't really think about it or plan for it? It is one of the most important callings of our lives, and to step into being a father without some help is foolish beyond words. We wouldn't have someone change our oil who had never thought about the process, so why would we think that something so important would just come naturally because we are there?

This book offers the genius of fellow fathers who have gone before you and asked the hard questions of themselves and others and then provided a clear and compelling vision of what it means to step into the glory and heartache that is ahead. It is about far more than diapers, late nights, and bad-tasting baby food. It is about cultivating a glorious new soul for the sake of the good things of life. You are in for a treat, and I can't wait to share with you the pictures of my children.

Dan B. Allender Ph.D
President, Mars Hill Graduate School
Author, *To Be Told* and *How Children Raise Parents*

ACKNOWLEDGEMENTS

It really is hard work writing a book. Many hours are spent simply typing word after word (half of which never get used). And for that, we get our names on the front. While that means we're the authors, it in no way means we get all the credit. We had a lot of help along the way.

First, we want to thank Relevant Books. This is an awesome company striving to make a difference. We are honored to be affiliated with an organization so committed to art with integrity, creativity, and excellence. Every step of the way, you've been gracious and enthusiastic. Specifically, we would like to thank Cameron for letting us have a voice; Cara for believing in us; Kyle, Summer, and Jeff for telling the story to others. You guys keep on doing what you're doing. It matters so much.

Secondly, we must express our deepest gratitude to Jana Mutsinger and her partner Pamela McClure at McClure/Muntsinger Public Relations. God has blessed us with some extraordinary gifts while we've worked on this book; Jana's gracious participation may be the best of all. We still can't believe you want to be a part of this. It is humbling.

Laura Armistead was a great help with the sidebars. Her humor, willingness, and hard work saved the day. Anything of value in the sidebars is her contribution.

We must thank The Frothy Monkey and Portland Brew: the official caffeine and dessert suppliers for this project. A lot of calories were consumed in the creation of this work (much more than were burned), and these places kept us

....

well supplied along the way.

Finally, let us not forget our Creator. How do we begin to thank a God who has loved us so much? Abba's willingness to lavish us with relationships, opportunities, and creativity is astonishing. His commitment and passion to transform our hearts amazes and humbles us. His desire for us is breathtaking. It is so great to be loved by a God who is far gentler with us than we deserve. We hope you know this love, too.

STEPHEN'S GRATITUDE

In the Scriptures, especially in the first testament, when someone would encounter God in a personally transformative way, he would erect an altar or monument. These most often were simple piles of stones, one heaped upon the other. For me (Stephen), this book is a monument in my story. It marks the juncture of so many different plots. And like all good stories, mine has a cast of characters who have been important contributors.

Very little, if anything, in this book is original. In every way, David and I stand in the footsteps of giants, people who have walked ahead of us blazing trails of faith, fatherhood, and family. Outside of my own experience, what probably most influenced my contributions to this work was my time at Mars Hill Graduate School. This is indeed a rare and special place in the world. I would have never even dreamed of writing this without the presence of Dan Allender, Heather Webb, and Kirk Webb in my life. I must also thank my MHGS cohorts with whom I lived life for a season: Clinton, Mark, Greg, Ken, John, Kay, and others: You all changed my life.

I am blessed to have wise men who are willingly investing in me and in my journey. Specifically, I want to thank Al

Andrews, Zach Brittle, Chip Dodd, John Marshall, and Mike Wussow. The character of these men is rare. Their candor, loyalty, and courage are qualities I long to have more of in my own life. The best part of writing this book was being with David Thomas. David, you are so much more than a co-author: You are the truest of friends. Fathering, writing, and rafting alongside you is an awesome privilege. Thank you for being willing to be yourself with me. The branches of your heart are heavy with the fruit of curiosity, empathy, courage, and care. Because of you, I'm a better person. You are a great man. I can't believe I get to call you a friend. (Connie, thank you for sharing your husband for the last year.)

My family has been really important in shaping my story. Thanks to my parents for loving me so much and valuing my heart. I always felt loved growing up. Mom, it blesses me to see you becoming more and more of who Christ has always wanted you to be. Your enthusiastic love of my wife and children is the greatest gift you've ever given me. Dad, thanks for coming to all those soccer games and for teaching me values like hard work, integrity, and humility. Neely, I can't believe we both finally grew up. You are a great sister, and you and Clay will be awesome parents. (I can't wait to meet your son.) And, finally, my in-laws, the Gobble clan. How could I have known that when I married Heather, I would get to be part of such a generous family?

I have the most amazing kids, and I most surely want to thank them, for forgiving my absences while I was writing this book. Emma Claire and Elijah, you'll never know how much I love you and what gifts you are in my life. You've changed me forever. For sure, you are instruments of God's grace and mercy.

Much of how special my children are is due to their mother, my wife, Heather. She is a wonderful woman who bears an unbelievable passion for her kids. She is one of the most brave, industrious, and loyal people I've ever met. (Oh, did I mention that she is beautiful? She's that, too.) Honey, thank you for believing in my passions and being willing to trust my desires. You've journeyed with me to the continent's edge and back again. Nothing I could say or do would express the appreciation I have for what burdens you've born on my behalf. I doubt I really even know how heavy a load you've carried. You are an extraordinary mother, an exceptional wife, and my closest friend. You've taught me more about what it means to be Christ than anyone else.

DAVID'S GRATITUDE

I have run enough marathons to know the value of having people standing along the side of the road yelling out my name. It is what sustains me when I want to stop and just lay down in the street. Thank you to the following people, some of whom have been there since the gun fired and others who were standing at mile twenty-two when I was weary and certain that I had nothing important left to give: John and Kendra Allen, who believed in this book before the first sentence was written, and are better friends than I deserve. Trace, for your words and for sharing in the journey of fatherhood with me. Eric, for being so curious and for your love of writing. Ruben and Jerry, for a long history of believing in me and standing with me. The Harvill and Kitchens families, for loving my family well as if you lived next door when you are hundreds of miles away. Dave and Julie, your creativity inspires and stirs me, as does your friendship. Belle, Holly and Peter, for relationship that is so familiar and comfortable, and for keeping me going with homemade ice cream. Al, for your humor, your wisdom, and your stories . . . your influence is so present throughout the pages of this book. Carter, for your presence in some of the most sacred moments in my journey. Andy, that your life speaks of your love for Christ and how that moves me.

To my staff and friends at Daystar Counseling Ministries. Melissa, thank you for inviting me to be a part of something so meaningful, for what I have learned and continue to learn from you. Sissy, for shared passions and a shared history that I am so grateful for. Pace, Pat, Jeremy, and Betsy, you are so much more than my colleagues. I am blessed to work with people that I enjoy so much and count as dear friends.

My incredible family: Dad, thank you for your investment in who I am. So much of my experience of fathering is rooted in being loved well by you. Thank you, also, for being the first person to believe I could write and for endless hours spent editing me. Mom, you have always been my biggest cheerleader. Thank you that our home was full of stories, creativity, and laughter. Sharon, for setting the standard for a sister and an aunt. Jim, for coming along at just the right time. Robert and Peggy, thank you for how you welcomed me into your life fifteen years ago and how you continue to do that. Bob and Amy, I am blessed to have inherited you as siblings and your children as my neices and nephew.

Stephen, I have learned so much about myself throughout the journey of creating this work. It all started with our first conversation about this book and your invitation to me. Thank you for believing that I had something worth saying. Your strength and courage continue to challenge and disrupt me. You are a brilliant writer, a passionate father, an intentional husband, and a great man. I'm thankful to have shared in this with you. Heather, thank you for your perspective and what you brought to this book. I am relieved that your husband is well aware that you are responsible for much of his greatness. Emma Claire and

Elijah, thank you for sharing your dad with me for such a long time. I am so glad that my kids have friends like the two of you.

Connie, how many times have you stood at the finish line while I ran, yelling out my name? Waking at the crack of dawn, standing in the cold and the rain, just to see me finish. You have outdone yourself this time. You have made great sacrifices to allow me to do something that I love. I don't even know how to thank you. Just know that I love you deeply. Thank you for staying in this with me. I am inspired and overwhelmed when I watch you with our children. I imagined it before we were ever married and I see it now the way I dreamed of it then. Someday, when our children's lives unfold into adulthood and they go on their way, I am thankful I get to finish with you.

Lily, Baker, and Witt, you three are the reasons I want to ask these questions again and again. You deserve a father who is deeply curious about his story, his heart, his marriage, and how he is loving you. You are gifts. "It's a great big world, it's a great big moon, it's a great big sky and a great big love for you."

"WAIT AND SEE WHERE THEY COME OUT."

— LATE NIGHT TALK SHOW HOST DAVID LETTERMAN
ADMONISHING FATHER-TO-BE KENNY ROGERS

INTRODUCTION

"Please remove all loose objects. Pull the harness over your head and fasten the buckle. The floor below you is about to drop. Enjoy your ride." Those were the last words spoken before being jarred, flipped, tossed, thrown, and thrust into the open. That's how my (David) experience on "Kracken" began. Kracken is named after a mythological sea monster that would attack ships at night and feed upon sailors. It's Orlando's fastest, largest, and only floorless coaster with a 144-foot drop, seven inversions, and a top speed of sixty-five miles per hour. One of the downhill cameras caught me with my mouth wide open, screaming with excitement and fear. I can still remember topping the first hill and that moment of being barely in motion before being thrust down the other side at light speed. The wildness of being flipped upside-down with my feet dangling in the sky, only to descend and be flipped again and again. (If I turn my head just slightly to the right, I can still feel it.)

I can also remember being seated in my kitchen with my wife sitting across from me. She slid a home pregnancy test across the table. Her eyes were enormous, and she could barely contain excitement as she waited for me to respond. I was breathless. I stared at the colored dot confirming our pregnancy and heard a voice say, "Pull the harness over your head and fasten the buckle. The floor below you is about to drop. Enjoy your ride."

The experiences were so similar. I spent the next nine months (as I have spent the last several years) being jarred, flipped, tossed, thrown, and thrust into the open. It was, and continues to be, a wild ride. A ride that I love with everything in me and one that scares the life out of me. A ride that I have absolutely no control of other than buckling up and pulling down the harness. I have spent the last years of my life with my mouth (sometimes literally) wide open, screaming with excitement and fear.

The difference is that within a matter of moments, Kracken came to a halt. The roller coaster edged up a bit, and I found myself in the place where I had started. I hit the buckle, and the harness lifted. I reconnected with my rhythm of breathing, and I exited the ride. This ride of fatherhood has no exit. It is still going and going and going, and I am still screaming with excitement and fear. Many days I still feel inverted and thrust into the unknown. In the midst of it all, I have a lot of questions about what in the world I am doing.

I (Stephen) remember when I found out my wife was pregnant. I recall thinking, *Oh, that's great. I'm ready for this*. I knew it was important. I suspected it would change my life. But I had no idea how much. By the way, neither do you. You may think you do, but you don't. I thought I did, but I didn't. I had no idea what was about to happen to me, to my marriage, to my relationship with my parents, to my relationships with my friends, to my relationship with my Creator.

My wife had been pregnant for about five months. We had heard the heartbeat, seen the ultrasound, and been to the doctor and a childbirth class. I felt prepared. I remember lying in bed with Heather talking about baby names, the nursery, birth announcements, and baby showers, and with love in her eyes, she said something to the effect of, "This is so wonderful." And then it hit me: I remember thinking, *Oh, #@%*$!!!! I'm going to be a dad!* I was so freaked out, I didn't sleep for three days.

WELCOME TO THE CLUB

Congratulations. If you're reading this book, chances are you're about to be or have just become a dad. And along with this new status, you've been ushered toward the most momentous threshold of your life.

We all come to this adventure from different places. You may be stepping into this exciting undertaking as the next phase of your family's master plan. Or, this might be the culmination of a long-fought journey full of hope and wrought with discouragement. For others, this news could have come unexpectedly and even perhaps unwantedly. Regardless of what brought you to this launching point in your story, you now find yourself thrust into mystery. You are hurling headlong toward one of the most impactful relationships you'll ever know—father and child. Hold on. It's a white-knuckled ride.

For all of us men, the most significant responsibility we may ever have is to join with our wives in creating life. Making babies is, in many ways, the fullest expression of our mark of divinity and is the explicit execution of our mandate to "fill and multiply." In Genesis it states:

> God created human beings
> He created them godlike;
> Reflecting God's nature.
> He created them male and female.
> He blessed them:
> "Prosper! Reproduce! Fill Earth! Take charge!
> Be responsible for fish in the sea and birds in the air,
> for every living thing that moves on the face of
> Earth." (Gen. 1:27-28, MSG)

Whatever else this time of expectation is (and it is full of a lot of things), for us as men, it brings us to a place of fulfilling our most central call and at the same time, takes us far beyond our grasp of control.

AN ANCIENT AND DIVINE CALL

There is a significant tie between full masculinity and fatherhood. Men are meant to be fathers, and those men who never know fatherhood firsthand will always ache in their experience of life. This in no way means that men who are not fathers are less manly. Nor does it mean that every man who becomes a father finds maturity, holiness, or wisdom. It does mean, however, that those men who do not have children miss out on the rich and abundant, life-altering blessings that come with being a father.

Fathers are important to God. The significance of the theme of fatherhood in Scripture cannot be overlooked. A common and pervasive expression of God's character in Scripture is that of Father. Many stories of God's faithfulness in Scripture hinge on God's paternal perspective.

Take a look at the first parents. If you read closely the account of Adam and Eve, you will notice that their encounter with God in the Garden did little to soften their hearts toward a deeper surrender to God. It is not until their children rebel, bleed, suffer, and die that Adam and Eve turn to God for help. It's not until Cain's rebellion that men begin to "call on the name of the Lord." Parenthood is expressly tied to holiness. And for us men, fatherhood is the door toward a return to our own hearts and God's heart.

Many of the stories throughout Scripture speak to the importance of fathers. There are only two sentences that describe Noah: the first as a righteous man, the second as a father (Gen. 6:9). Abraham's promise of being a great nation ("I will make your offspring like the dust of the earth" Gen. 13:16) was tied to his paternity; Abraham and Isaac's relationship was a cauldron for faith (Gen. 22). Wisdom Literature contains dozens of references to father/child relationships, and, when Satan attempted to drive Job to despair, he killed his children. The Gospels, too, are rich with the significant role a father plays. Even Jesus' Messiahship was confirmed by His paternal line from the royal House of David. When Christ wanted to paint a picture of God's endless mercy and power to forgive, He told of a father and son's reunion (Prodigal Son).

So why all this emphasis on fathers? What does God have in mind? God's desire for parenthood in general, and fatherhood specifically, is sanctification—making us more mature, wise, and loving. Parenthood, at its best, drives us to great surrender and dependency on God and uncovers the unique image of God we all bear.

PREPARATION AND EXPECTATION

We could try to describe in detail what the birth of your child and becoming a father will be like, but in truth, no words can give justice to the transformation in which you find yourself. It's like moving from one country to another, or more accurately, one planet to another. Whether this is your first child or second or third or fourth, this experience will forever shape you. You are being changed.

This year in the U.S., approximately 4 million babies will be born (National Center for Health Statistics). Many men report feelings of anxiety, confusion, and lack of preparation for the process of pregnancy and the reality of fatherhood. Becoming a parent is without a doubt a life-changing experience. It's a journey of transformation.

If a man is courageous enough to enter into this mysterious season, he will lay the groundwork for becoming an exceptional father, a passionate husband, and a wiser man. Fatherhood is so much more than changing diapers, or even making a living. Being a dad has more to do with bravely facing the deep questions of your soul than mastering the mechanics of baby care. (Although that's really important, too.)

I (David) remember watching my wife deliver our first child. To see her move into the process of delivery with purpose and intention was beautiful. Even with it being her first time, she responded so naturally. That's not to say there weren't awkward and painful moments. There were both. Yet, my wife was connected and engaged in the process. It was stunning to watch and be a part of it.

I, on the other hand, was a clumsy outsider waiting to be prompted and directed. I needed consistent instruction and required a great deal of coaching by the medical staff on hand. The only thing that came naturally to me was my awkwardness. Every part in my participation seemed to involve questions. Should I stand here? How do we breathe now? Is the contraction over? What do you need from me, honey? How much longer? I was clueless.

Many Questions

Thinking back on that experience now, I know I was asking so many things in my heart in addition to the things I was asking aloud. Am I needed here? Do I have the strength to be present with my wife while she labors in intense pain? Can I love this woman well? Am I prepared for what we are doing?

These are the deeper questions of the soul. We believe they are some of the same questions you are asking as well. Perhaps you are reading this book and preparing for the arrival of your first child. Maybe you already have a child, or it could be you and your spouse have just discussed the possibility of having children. Regardless of where you are along the spectrum, there are questions stirring within you. We want to help you to ask them out loud. We encourage you to bring them to your spouse, other men, and God. We want to help you connect with them in a real way. We believe that wrestling aloud with these questions will equip you to engage with your heart. The outcome of a man who is engaged with his heart is a man who is postured to love his wife well, to pour into his children, to care for the people in his world, and to worship his God.

Because you have this book in your hand, you are somewhere in that place yourself. You just may not even know it. Or maybe you know it, and no one has helped you put words to it. You may be months into a pregnancy and find yourself anticipating it one moment and freaking out the next. You may have already become a father for the first, second, or third time. If so, you are aware that the floor below you is about to drop. Wherever you are in the midst of it, congratulations! You are somewhere in the most transforming, redemptive, exposing, life-altering experience of your existence.

There are many books that have been written for fathers with ideas about what to take to the hospital, dating after birthing, and managing finances on a limited income. These are important topics to discuss and ones that deserve attention. We encourage you to read these books. However, in talking with many new fathers, it is clear these books lack the spiritual and emotional underpinnings needed to adequately address the deep questions that are swimming in the heart of every man. This book is for the expectant or new father who desires to become more invested with his child, his marriage, his life, and his story. It will help you get ready for the disruptive experience called fatherhood. This book is centered on ten questions that every man must face in order to succeed as a father.

- **Do I want to become a father?**

- **Am I as happy as she is?**

- **Am I ready?**

- **Is this really happening?**

- **Will my wife love the baby more than me?**

- **What if my house is too small?**

- **What if I screw up another person's life?**

- **What if something terrible happens to my child?**

- **How do I prepare?**

- **What do I do now?**

In addition to asking these questions, we offer many practical suggestions for first-time dads. We also have some helpful ideas to pass on to you around everything from sex with your wife to personal finances. We provide a relational model of authentic fatherhood and masculinity. Our desire is to offer you the necessary relational tools, appropriate information, and technical skills needed throughout fatherhood.

Rollercoasters are designed to scare you to death and have you love it at the exact same time. The downhill camera captures you in that moment of intense excitement and fear. God created fatherhood to be similarly thrilling. God is writing your story so that you will be transformed and exposed in order to reveal His glory. He is using the vehicle of fatherhood to reclaim your heart, your desires, your fear, your hope, your passion, your uncertainty, and everything else in you. It's a wild ride!

It's a vehicle to some of the greatest pleasure in your life and fear like you've never felt before. It can shape you more into the image of your Maker and posture you to cry out to God. Children have the power to take us to some of the most glorious and painful places. So be warned. "Remove all loose objects. Pull the harness over your head and fasten the buckle. The floor below you is about to drop. Enjoy your ride."

"Ours is a world where people don't know what they want and are willing to go through hell to get it."

—Don Marquis

CHAPTER 1
Do I Want to Be a Father?

Mike was twenty-six. After three years of marriage, he and his wife Sarah had just purchased their first house—a charming three-bedroom starter home in a subdivision of charming three-bedroom starter homes. Mike had recently received a big promotion at work, which came with a good raise. The holidays were around the corner, and he and Sarah were looking forward to celebrating with friends and family. For the first time as an adult, Mike began to feel like he had life figured out. All was right with the world. He felt safe, secure, and in charge.

One Monday evening after work, Mike and Sarah met for dinner at a local restaurant. Mike was wiped out. He had finished negotiating his first deal at work since his promotion. He felt more relieved than celebratory. He was looking forward to eating with Sarah and then retreating home to catch the second half of Monday Night Football. But from the moment he met Sarah in the parking lot, he could tell that something was on her mind.

"Mike," she began after their drinks were ordered, "do you ever think about having a baby?"

Now, while Mike and Sarah had only been married for a season, he knew enough by this point to know that his next sentence could determine the rest of the evening. It wasn't that this was a subject he wanted to avoid, as much as it was that he would have picked something else to talk about. He chose to be affirmative but not committal—a tactic he played by often.

"Sure I do," Mike said with a grin, trying to catch the score of the game over his wife's shoulder.

"What do you think?" Sarah wondered.

"Sorry, what?" He was watching the replay.

"When you think of having kids, what do you think?"

Obviously being noncommittal was the wrong play. Mike knew changing the subject would be hurtful to Sarah, but maybe he could try turning the tables.

"It'll be great to be a dad one day. What about you? Do you think about it a lot?" *All right!* he thought. *The Dolphins just scored.*

"Mike, I think I'm ready," Sarah said.

"Sure, honey. I'll get the waitress so we can order," Mike said as he waved at their waitress across the room.

"No, Mike. I am ready for a baby." Sarah paused. "Do you want to have a baby?"

Sarah's question hung in the air just as the waitress stepped up to the table.

"Do you know what you want?" the waitress asked. "Can I take your order?"

Mike was panicked—his mind rushing with thoughts. He and Sarah had talked about having kids off and on since they started dating. Of course he wanted children. And when he would drive by a Saturday morning soccer game, he would occasionally dream about coaching a son one day. Many of his friends were having babies. His younger brother's wife was expecting in a few months. Sarah's sister had had a baby last year. He had even used the idea of children one day as a way of motivating Sarah to buy the new house. For him, it was still an idea. But he could tell that for Sarah, it was more than an idea. Much more. His heart knew what his brain could not articulate—she was full of hope, and her heart swelled with desire. The deepest parts of her longed for a child. His racing mind came to a screeching halt.

"Sir. Do you know what you want?" It was the waitress. "Do you want me to come back in a few minutes?"

"No. I guess I'm ready," Mike said. "I think I'll have . . . a burger and fries."

He knew the moment the waitress left, he was going to have to answer Sarah's question. As the waitress turned away, she smiled at Sarah in a way that made Mike feel uneasy.

There was a silence between Mike and his wife. Was she waiting him out? It was his turn to speak. She had asked him a question. Mike had learned at a sales seminar that when negotiating, the first to speak always loses. Did Sarah know this too? *She must,* he thought.

"Sarah," Mike started, and the moment he did, he knew that his life, his marriage, and his future were unalterably changed. "Do you want to have a baby?" But of course he knew the answer. And before they left the restaurant that night, they had agreed to start trying to have a baby. Mike was going to be a father; not tomorrow, not next week, probably not even in the next nine months, but sometime in the not too distant future, Mike was going to be called "Dad."

Do you want to have a baby? Do you want to be a father? What if the answer to those question is "no" for you? Or what if the answer is "no" in some moments and "yes" in other moments? While your response goes back and forth, your wife's response may at all times be "yes." If it is sometimes yes and sometimes no, don't worry. You're normal. It is part of a man's journey to answer this question with mixed responses. Most men feel both excited and terrified at the idea of becoming a father.

I (Stephen) recall the season when my wife and I were trying to get pregnant for the first time. We had been attempting to get pregnant for a couple of months, and I remember feeling more fearful that we would get pregnant than worried that we wouldn't. As a father, I am sometimes confident in my journey and at other times paralyzed with feelings of self-doubt that say, "What was I thinking in becoming a dad?"

There were many moments of questioning. I knew that everything in my wife wanted to create life. And at the same time, only some part of me, maybe not even much of me, wanted that same thing. I was hiding. I remember asking myself the question, "What is wrong with you?" I had a beautiful wife and a healthy, growing marriage. We had always discussed wanting to have children. So how could I get four years into marriage and suddenly decide that I had no desire to have a kid?

It wasn't until sometime after my first child was born that I came to realize that I was asking a much deeper question of myself. The ambivalence of fatherhood was really about another question—a question I believe I had been asking myself for the past twenty years. It is a question every man is asking throughout his life.

It is a question we men ask ourselves, our Creator, our fathers, our wives, and other people in our life. It is a question of validation. It's the question every boy asks the first time he steps up to the plate and brings the bat back over his shoulder in preparation to swing. It's the question every teenage boy asks when presented with the opportunity to invite a girl to prom. It's the question every young man asks when he steps onto a college campus for the first time. It's the question every professional asks when the sales figures roll in and quarterly reports are presented. It's the same question I asked when I felt frozen by fear in the face of becoming a father: Do I have what it takes?

Do I have what is required to come through? If the bases are loaded and I'm up to bat, can I pull out a hit? Is she interested enough in me to respond by saying, "Yes"? Can I make the grades? Do I want to be a father? They are all different versions of the same question: Do I have what it takes?

A great film by John Hughes that showcases the new father's experience is *She's Having a Baby*. It's the story of a young couple, Jake (Kevin Bacon) and Kristy (Elizabeth McGovern) Briggs. The movie begins with their wedding day and chronicles their relationship through the birth of their first child. Hilarious and poignant, the film is a window to Jake's heart and his insecurities. In one central scene, Jake and Kristy are lying in bed following a stressful dinner with their parents.

Kristy:	Are you mad?
Jake:	No.
Kristy:	Would you rather not talk?
Jake:	I'm fine. What do you want to talk about?
Kristy:	You know.
Jake:	Kids? You want kids?
Kristy:	Don't you?
Jake:	It's irreversible.
Kristy:	So?
Jake:	I'm not in the mood for an irreversible action right now. Let's go to sleep. Having our parents here . . . started everything. It's not a good time to talk serious. Go to sleep. *Long pause.*
Kristy:	If I tell you something, will you promise not to get mad?
Jake:	What is it?

Kristy:	Promise you won't get mad?
Jake:	Tell me what it is?
Kristy:	You have to promise you won't get mad.
Jake:	Okay. I promise I won't get mad.
Kristy:	I stopped taking the pill three months ago.
Jake:	Aah! (*Jake envisions himself strapped in a seat flying into a wall*).

Like Jake, many of us are ambivalent with the prospect of becoming a dad. Asking the question, "Do I want to be a father?" calls forth a collage of feelings: hope, frustration, joy, incompetence, fear, anticipation, arousal, shame, dejection, anxiety, anger, rejection, humiliation, guilt, excitement, sadness, loneliness. If we are honest about our hearts, it is with positive-uncertainty that most of us consider the idea of fatherhood. Many men respond to the idea of having a baby with an ambivalence that says, "I guess I'm ready."

What is it then about the prospect of being a dad that is so unnerving? For most of us men, fatherhood, more than any other relationship, exposes how limited and needy we are. At the heart of every man is the seed of self-doubt that nags at his ego, "Do I have what it takes?" Nowhere is this more true than in the realm of marriage and fatherhood, because nowhere else in our lives are our imperfections and incompleteness more exposed.

It takes bold courage for us as men to begin to ask and ultimately face this, the most exposing of questions. To honestly ask and begin answering the question, "Do I want to be a father?" is to face the reality that you might not have what it takes. It exposes your heart to the uncomfortable reality that your greatest emotional and spiritual fears are true: You are not enough.

THE FACE OF GOD REVEALED

Being a dad is a big deal. A child's connection (or the lack of one) with his/her father is for sure one of life's most defining experiences. The first glimpse of God children encounter is the face of their parents. As fathers, we possess tremendous power to bless or curse our children. If it has happened already, you will find yourself standing godlike over your child, awestruck by the expectations and responsibilities this precious and fragile life demands.

Being a father is the most important thing you will ever do. No matter how high on the corporate ladder you climb, "Dad" is the most powerful title you will every wear. It was this same paternal tie that set us each off in our own unique directions as men. It defined us and shaped us like the first blows of the sculptor into the granite—calling forth the image within. Scripture is clear: You bear the mark of God. With that marking comes responsibility.

On an absolutely physiological level, children cannot escape the impact of their fathers. Science tells us that it is the father's chromosome alone that determines sex. DNA embedded in the genetic code that is passed from the father helps determine if the child is brown-eyed or blue, red-haired or black, thin or fat, short or tall, anxious or laid back, prone to high blood pressure or alcoholism—the list goes on and on and on. And on another level, the quality and depth of our relationships with our own fathers influences every part of our lives: from how we relate to God to how we relate to our wives; from how we see ourselves to how we relate with other men; and for certain, how we relate to our own children.

Picture your father's face. Can you see it? His smile. His anger. His laugh. His disappointment. His pride. These images are branded on the flesh of your heart and have the power to evoke many emotions. I (Stephen) can easily remember the comforting smell of my father's cologne as he drove me to elementary school in his brown Lincoln. I can still see him proudly waiting at the gate of the field following a high school game. I will never forget the feeling of his arms holding me upright as I (a grown man) wept into his chest at the funeral of a boyhood friend.

It's A Big Deal

Fatherhood is an awesome responsibility and experience. The feelings of fear and awe at being a father are well founded. By all accounts, it is loaded with more joy and heartache than you could ever dare to dream about experiencing. There is little that is more affirming than being enthusiastically greeted at the door by your son when you arrive home. There are fewer moments as sweet as dancing with your daughter while she stands on your feet. Not much can measure up to the perfect simplicity of an afternoon with your family in the park. Few meals taste as rich as Saturday morning pancakes with your kids. Similarly, you will never hurt as deeply as when your child experiences the sting of rejection. The taste of injustice will never be as unpalatable as when your child is overlooked. Terror will never be as present as when the pediatrician says, "We need to run a few tests."

Being an Excellent Father

In order to become an excellent father, men need to be committed to growing in maturity, wisdom, and love. To accomplish this growth, men must be willing to be risky, vulnerable, and passionate. No, we are not talking about being effeminate. Masculinity is an essential quality of fatherhood, and it takes a very brave man to be an excellent father. The challenge is that wisdom, maturity, and love are born out of brokenness, surrender, and desire.

Most guys in their twenties and early thirties have not been broken by life. They have most certainly been bumped and bruised, but it is rare that a younger man has confronted the brutality of life and loss. It is not a fault, but rather the way God tends to write our stories. Unless a man's life is marked by unnatural tragedy or violence, early adulthood is a time of ambition, energy, creation, and construction. It is some time in this period that men come to face reality. Life is hard. And somehow, for many men, God uses becoming a father as a significant portal to greater maturity, wisdom, and love. He softens our hearts for His glory.

The process of fathering is designed to be a transforming one. It is intended to be disruptively redemptive. Its purposes are to expose and sanctify the human heart and reveal the glory of God.

So Why Fight It?

One reason many men are resistant to answering the question, "Do I want to be a father?" is because they know that as Jake Briggs said, "it's an irreversible action." Everything in a man's life changes when he becomes a dad: what he wears, where he goes, what he drives, how he spends his free time, how he spends his money, when he can have sex with his wife, how long he can sleep, if he can use the bathroom in private. There is no escaping the effects of becoming a Dad.

I (David) remember finding out that our "second" child was really two children in my wife's womb. The news of twins sent us spinning. We were living in a thousand-square-foot house, and I was driving a Nissan Sentra. Everything fit just right for our small family of three, but now we were becoming a family of five. Within moments of our first discussion about upgrading our vehicle to accommodate three car seats, the word "minivan" crept into our conversation. I felt a sick feeling in my stomach. I tried desperately to convince my wife that purchasing a minivan would involve selling my soul. I imagined myself driving about town in my seven-passenger shack on wheels with my confidence blowing out the exhaust.

It's a done deal. I am now the proud owner of a Nissan Quest minivan. It was an irreversible action. For me, it involved giving in to the whole package. The reality is that I may never drive a sports car . . . or even a "non-family" car again (at least not for the next decade or two).

GET REAL

This world is full of men who aren't living out of their hearts. You don't have to go very far to encounter a man who is disconnected from his heart. A man whose wife feels lonely in relationship with him, whose kids feel neglected or overlooked, whose coworkers feel used, whose friends feel estranged. Perhaps you don't have to look outside your own house to find that man. As therapists, we see that man every day in our offices. If we don't meet with him individually, we listen to his son talk about longing to be with him, or we sit with his wife while she cries about missing him. Take a look around. You will see him, too. Either you know him, or you are him.

Do you want to be a father? Probably you do . . . and you don't. It's likely that the idea of it stirs a number of things in you. We know it does in us. But perhaps a better question is, do you have the courage to connect with what it stirs in you, or will you pretend it's not there? Will you be courageous enough to name all the things you feel when you entertain the idea of fathering? Will you buy into the idea that this disruptive, exposing process will transform you? Will you ask these questions aloud and believe that it will be beneficial for you, your wife, and your children? It's your call. If you choose to do it, you will discover that the initial investment reaps a lifetime of rewards. By doing so, you are setting a tone in your life, your work, and your family. You will also discover that it demands courage and creativity, but so do most things worthwhile.

Learn the Names of Your Wife's Private Parts

Your wife has parts that you haven't yet discovered, and as she grows throughout her pregnancy, you need to have a clear understanding of what her body is doing. Here is a refresher course on female anatomy:

- **VAGINA**—A muscular tunnel that connects the external genitals to the uterus. The vaginal walls are moist, elastic, and muscular and can stretch to various sizes, as you will see during delivery. The vagina is self-cleaning, periodically shedding mucus and dead cells as discharge, which will increase during pregnancy.

- **UTERUS**—a hollow muscular pear-shaped organ where the baby develops. It is normally about the size of a fist, but expands during pregnancy.

- **CERVIX**—the lowest part of the uterus that keeps the growing embryo inside; contains mucus-producing glands that keep bacteria out of the uterus and help sperm enter the uterus when the egg is ripe.

- **MUCUS PLUG**—produced by mucus-producing glands in the cervix at the opening of the uterus to protect the baby from infection.

- **ISTHMUS**—middle section of the uterus that lengthens during pregnancy.

- **CORPUS**—upper muscular section of the uterus.

- **ENDOMETRIUM**—lining of the uterus that holds and nourishes a developing fetus.

- **PLACENTA**—attaches the baby to the inside of the uterus; blood vessels in the placenta join to form the umbilical cord, which attaches to your baby at the belly button. The umbilical cord delivers oxygen and nutrition and carries away waste.

- **FALLOPIAN TUBES (2)**—passageways connecting the uterus and ovaries where the egg cells develop.

- **OVARIES (2)**—female sex glands that produce eggs (ova) and the hormones estrogen and progesterone, which control the ripening and releasing of the eggs.

Nurturing the Nurturer

Whenever experienced parents discover that you're expecting, they always tell you how having a baby will change your life. It's true! It changes you both as individuals and as a couple. You may find that you are sometimes at an impasse with your wife, waiting for her to meet your needs while she waits for you to meet hers. At those times, it is important for you to take the lead and love sacrificially.

• Encourage your wife to rest, maybe napping when the baby does. Send her to bed early while you watch the baby. It's amazing what sleep can do for your wife.

• Jump in when it comes to caring for the baby. Take initiative and don't wait to be asked to change a dirty diaper.

• Pray with her and for her regularly. She is constantly giving out as she cares for the baby and will need spiritual refreshment.

• Help her find time alone when she doesn't have to meet anyone's needs but her own.

• Plan date times when you are alone together to reconnect and grow your relationship.

• Give her time to do the things that she is passionate about outside of motherhood. It will rejuvenate her.

• Communicate about your wants, needs, dreams, etc. Although you have become parents, you are a couple first. It is important for you to discuss your feelings about your new life—what you love, what is hard, what would be helpful—and hear your spouse's perspective. Remember that you're on the same team!

"MEN CAN FORGET [THAT THEIR WIVES ARE PREGNANT] FOR HOURS ON END, AND IT IS OUR JOB TO KEEP THAT FROM HAPPENING. DON'T EVER LET HIM LABOR UNDER THE DELUSION THAT GESTATING IS PART-TIME WORK."

—VICKI LOVINE
GIRLFRIEND'S GUIDE TO PREGNANCY

CHAPTER 2
AM I AS HAPPY AS SHE IS?

We have it on video: the exact moment Heather and I (Stephen) learned she was pregnant with our first child. It's captured forever: the elation, the shock, the gratefulness, the doubt, the awe.

A few weeks earlier, we had taken a week-long trip to a secluded cabin on the fringe of a rugged national park. We carefully timed this excursion with a singular goal: making a baby. Not quite two weeks later, we found ourselves sitting on our bathroom floor waiting for the home pregnancy test to reveal an answer that would forever change our lives.

Heather had deemed it bad luck to watch the test develop. She figured this could somehow skew the results. So the pregnancy test rested out of sight on the vanity while we leaned against the tub opposite the video camera talking about the glorious "what ifs" for three excruciatingly long minutes. Unlike the Magic 8-Ball, this device would render a decisive "yes" or "no." There would be no ambiguous, "maybe" or, "the future is unclear." In a matter of moments, we would know our course.

The footage we shot reveals a bewildered couple full of hope. I was obviously restless, glancing at my watch every fifteen seconds certain the three minutes had expired.

"Do you think you're pregnant?" I asked.

"Surely not. It usually takes months of trying to get pregnant," Heather replied, hedging her bet. Part of me hoped she was right. This being only our second month of trying, the odds were against it. On average, it takes six to eight months to conceive, and many doctors won't even recommend medical intervention until a couple has tried for at least a year. My heart pounded with expectation. What would the test reveal? Yes or no? One line or two? Plus or minus? Baby or not?

I decided to try to lower my expectations so as not to be disappointed. I have a sketchy record with tests, as proven through years of high school mediocrity. Give me an essay, and I'm fine, but any other type of assessment, and I'm up a creek. (Heck, I barely passed the written driver's exam.) Why should I think this test would be any different? Granted, there is very little I could do to mess this up. There aren't too many different ways to pour a cup of urine onto a plastic stick.

In reality, pregnancy tests are quite simple, but to look at the lengthy directions that come with them, you would think you are trying build a rocket to the moon. Ours had eight pages of small type in both English and Spanish. While tests vary somewhat, fundamentally, they're similar. The woman pees in a cup. Apparently, the cup needs to be clean. (To me, this seemed oxymoronic—pouring pee into a clean cup—but my wife assured me it was important.) Next, you pour the urine onto the test stick and wait. Many women claim the hardest part is getting the urine onto the stick. I disagree. The hardest part is waiting the three minutes it takes to develop the test. I am pretty convinced that is what all the directions are for—to fill your time while you wait.

"Should we look?" I asked.

"No. It hasn't been three minutes," Heather chided.

"When can we look?"

"When it's time," she insisted.

A lot can go through your head in three minutes, but even

more can transpire in your heart. Recently, re-watching the video of this moment reminded me of the waves of excitement, dread, joy, uncertainty, faith, insecurity, and love that washed through my soul as we waited.

And finally the time came. We rose, picked up the video camera, and walked across the bathroom to ascertain our destiny. Who knew that a little urine and a PH stick could bear so much meaning? Surely not me.

"Oh my goodness! We're pregnant!" I exclaimed.

"Are you sure?" she asked.

"It's a plus!" I responded, but we compared our test stick to the illustration in the directions several times to make certain. There was no doubt about it—we were going to have a baby. We stood there in the bathroom for a few more moments, embracing each other, humbled and overjoyed by the gift with which God chose to bless us.

As that moment of ecstatic discovery eroded away over the next few hours, days, and weeks, I grew increasingly disengaged. I found myself going to work earlier and staying later filling my time with "projects." I increasingly forgot that Heather was pregnant, only to be surprised in moments of remembering when reality would pounce on me from behind. There were moments working at my desk when the full weight of the approaching responsibility would drop on me like a piano.

As autumn arrived, I grew quietly resentful of Heather's pleasure in her approaching motherhood. Certainly part of me was glad about the prospect of becoming a father, but I was in no way as happy as Heather. Was there something wrong with me?

There is another similar scene in *She's Having a Baby*. Jake and Kristy have attempted getting pregnant for a long stretch. They have endured fertility tests, monitored her temperature religiously, and practiced conception-friendly techniques. Jake enters his office one morning and is stopped by the receptionist who informs him that his wife called and wants to meet him downtown at 5:00 p.m. at the Museum of Natural History. We then find Jake walking slowly through the Museum toward his wife. She is seated in front of a fountain regarding him. As he comes to her, she stands and stares into him.

> **Kristy:**   Jake, we're going to have a baby.
> *Long pause (she smiles as she looks at him).*
> I found out this morning, and I didn't want to tell you on the phone.
> *Pause.*
> How do you feel?
> *Silence.*
> Are you as happy as I am?
> *Pause (he smiles awkwardly).*
> **Jake:**   I think so . . . yeah. Yeah.
> *They embrace. The camera looks over her shoulder at Jake's face. His eyes are full of panic. The camera then shows her face. She is smiling with joy and contentment.*
> **Kristy:**   We're blessed.
> *Jake stares with continued fear.*

At this point, the song "Apron Strings" quietly breaks in. The words are heard again and again. *Apron Strings, apron strings, I want someone to tie to my apron strings.* We see Kristy seated on the bed rubbing her stomach and smiling with delight. The contrast is astounding. Her delight, his panic. Her joy, his fear. Her excitement, his hesitation. From the moment he approaches her in the museum, we feel his hesitancy. We see it in his slow approach and the blank stare on his face. We feel it in the long silence following her words. We hear it as Jake struggles to answer the question: "Are you as happy as I am?"

A Step Behind?

It isn't uncommon to hear the sentence, "Boys mature slower than girls." We could walk into almost any kindergarten across the country and see that statement played out. It speaks to the reality that there is typically a lag in the emotional development of a boy that is noticeably different when comparing him to his female classmates. The gap can continue to get larger as a boy develops. It explains some of why girls often find themselves attracted to guys one to two years older by the time they reach high school. Older boys tend to be more of an emotional match in this season of development. This phenomenon can remain in place into adulthood.

How might this play itself out in the arena of fatherhood? Could it be that men are actually excited about what is taking place, but our excitement comes at a later stage and looks quite different? Is it possible that we feel the point of impact a little differently or further down the road?

For those of you reading this book who are already fathers, can you remember back to the earliest moments and weeks of your child's life? Can you remember your spouse bonding physically and emotionally with your infant and feeling on the outside of that?

I (David) remember seeing my wife nurse all three of our children and saying to myself, "I have absolutely nothing to offer this person. My wife is capable of meeting my child's every need. All that my baby wants can be found in one person." Some of these thoughts and feelings continued well into the first seasons of my children's lives. I still feel it at times. Yet I can also remember a time when I felt I did have something unique and needed to offer.

I had a conversation with a couple who experienced a miscarriage in their first trimester. The husband spoke of how he couldn't empathize with his wife's sadness. He felt sadness himself, but nothing like what his wife experienced. We talked of how connected she was with their pregnancy from the earliest moments. Life was growing in *her* body, and life would pass from *her* body. For this man, he had yet to really connect with a life that he could not see, feel, or touch.

This can continue to be the case for a man throughout the early years of parenting. A woman can feel connected in ways that we don't. Not only can she carry a child, she can be the sole food source. Every physical need can be met in infancy by the mother. Not to mention the emotional needs. With our own children, we find them calling out one name most often when they are hurt, scared, or sad. The name "Mommy" is the most spoken word in our homes. How do we build connection when we don't sense a need? Often, we men feel inferior and incapable in comparison to our wives when it comes to parenthood.

A DIFFERENT DESIGN

We believe men are not hard-wired to function in this arena the same as women. Men tend to be action-oriented. God's initial instruction to the first man was to "'be fruitful and increase in number; fill the earth and subdue it. Rule over the fish of the sea and the birds of the air and every other living creature that moves on the ground.'" (Gen. 1: 28). As men, we innately understand the process of being fruitful and multiplying. We have a sense of our role in leading, naming, and working. Work for many of us is where we feel most confident, secure, and productive (and subsequently, where we feel most comfortable with ourselves).

As fathers, we often stumble into this process of nurturing. From a man's perspective, pregnancy and early fatherhood seem passive. This season calls for very little action. It feels outside of our design. This is foreign to how we men are created. As men, we are wired for events. It is often only through external occurrences that we are open to responding to our internal reality.

This action orientation is a far cry from the process of pregnancy and early fatherhood. If everything goes well, pregnancy is not action-packed. In my memory (Stephen), the moments I most vividly recall are events: conception, waiting at the OBGYN's office, hearing the baby's heartbeat, seeing the ultrasound, the onset of labor, the managed chaos of birth. The thing I found most frustrating about many of these events is that they called forth very little response from me. There was nothing for me to do.

For the most part, my daughter's birth was near textbook perfect. My wife went into labor. I rushed home. We went to the hospital. Early the next morning, the doctor handed us a beautiful baby girl. Everything went according to plan. In contrast, my son's birth was marked with calamity. Labor happened horrifyingly quickly, and my wife and son teetered for many moments between life and death. However, in myriad ways, his birth, while scary and unpredictable, was much more rewarding for me. For a long time, this confounded and shamed me, until I realized that my son's birth required my participation beyond being a "supportive birth partner." It demanded that I become actively engaged in the practice of saving lives. I wouldn't say that I *enjoyed* his birth more than my daughter's (that would be morbid), yet, I can say with certainty that I felt much more masculine and in many ways, oddly more comfortable.

Before pregnancy and parenthood, life has its own predictable rhythm. Monday through Friday comes and goes. Saturday and Sunday slow a bit until Monday rolls around again. Despite life's inevitable tragedies and touchdowns, time goes by in a familiar orderliness. When pregnancy hits, time unpredictably lurches and lunges— accelerating and decelerating. One day you comfortably ask yourself, "When will this baby get here?" Another day it's, "Oh, man! We only have a couple of months left?" Men often go long stretches forgetting our wives are pregnant, only to be yanked back into reality by a friend's inquiry about our burgeoning spouses.

The predictable inactivity of pregnancy opens the way for many of us men to seem less enthused than our wives. On the contrary, once you have children, life hits overdrive, and time accelerates exponentially. All of the sudden, life races away in a blur of activity. Overnight, everything changes: your schedule, your priorities, your marriage, your finances, your responsibilities. These are changes to which we find it hard to adjust. Life, while now full of action, is not about us. This can be hard to take.

Becoming a father transforms your priorities, your expectations, and your perceptions of the world. You are ultimately amazed by your capacity for love and your willingness to hate. Then you find yourself asking this question: "What is wrong with me?"

I (David) find myself asking this question on a regular basis, like when I find myself in the Krispy Kreme drive-thru fifteen minutes after completing a workout (the neon hot sign illuminating my dashboard and the sweat on my brow). Or when I order a white monkey mocha with an extra shot of banana syrup and then ask the barista to use skim milk. What am I thinking? The question comes to mind every time I train for a marathon and moan my way through the long runs. I realize that the body was not made to run 26.2 miles without pain and extreme discomfort. I consider a similar question each time I pack three active toddlers on an airplane and wrangle them until I want to release the ejection door and jump. Why am I doing this? What is wrong with me?

I have asked these questions even more frequently since becoming a father. I remember taking my firstborn into the doctor at eight days old and hearing our pediatrician diagnose her with RSV, a potentially deadly virus. Days into a hospital stay and hearing a monitor sound off every time her heartrate fluctuated, I wept, asking why we had submitted ourselves to this kind of love for a child and vulnerability of life. I remember potty training that same little girl at two and the challenge of mastering "poop in the potty." It would end up anywhere but in the toilet.

Months into the process and dozens of accidents later, I found myself cleaning it out of the bathtub one day, thinking what is wrong with me that I want to leave town, escape my wife and family, and never come home. I have had many more days like that in the past years . . . many more than I'd like to confess. Days where my heart was polluted with thoughts so dark that (in the words of Anne Lamott) "they would make Jesus want to drink gin out of a cat dish."

I do an amazing job of thinking about myself. I'm good at it—really good! I don't think about my wife so naturally, or my kids as often as I would choose. My wife is different.

Just this afternoon, she left to have some time for herself. Time away from the kids and a chance to be alone is rare and sacred. She had only been gone for half an hour when she called to say she was at the health-food store picking up a particular item that my sons love to eat, then she was headed over to get coffee and think about ideas for the kids' upcoming birthday parties. I thought to myself, *When I get an afternoon off, the last thing you will find me doing is buying kid-friendly foods at the store and dreaming about birthdays, unless it's my own.* Even when away, she is engaged in her role as mother. It is what she loves, who she is, and where she most desires to be. So, "What's wrong with me?"

Do you know this question? Do you ever feel these kinds of moments? Have you ever asked the question or some variation of it? Maybe you never asked that question before and you did feel excitement in the moment, possibly for some time afterwards. And then the tide turned, and you found yourself on the other side of excitement. Joy gave way to fear. Delight relocated, and panic established residency in its place. Or maybe you faked a response of enthusiasm when asked the question. You knew better than to stare with a blank expression as Jake did, and you gave it your best performance. Yet underneath, your heart was screaming, "I'm not happy—I'm terrified or angry or sad or _____."

You are likely somewhere in this scene. If you allow for any truth to rise from your heart, you will probably confirm that you have been there before, or you are there right now. Where do you go at this point? Only in acknowledging how you've lived on the fringes will you be able to join more fully.

Am I Happy?

With all the unfathomable gifts and glory that being a parent brings, it is also crowded with considerable loss and disruption. For us men to successfully transition into fatherhood, we need to inventory the things that parenthood robs from us. Not until we count the cost of our losses will we be truly able to appreciate and accept the value of the gifts inherent in fatherhood.

The search for joy is a big part of life. Pleasure and contentment are core desires of the human heart. Scientific discoveries in human brain research over the last twenty-five years have revealed that we are chemically hardwired for two basic rewards: food and sex.[1] There are more nerve receptors in the human mouth and genitalia than any other parts of the body. We are biologically designed to seek pleasure and avoid pain. More simply put, we are made by God for joy. This is true whether we are talking in emotional, spiritual, or physical terms.

If we are made for joy, why do we so often settle for getting by? Why are our lives filled with addictions, compulsions, disorders, and anxieties? Why do we work so hard for approval and acceptance? Why does shame tie us to the moorings of isolation and depression? Why do we feel so alone and empty-hearted so much of the time? It seems that God has placed us in a bind: If we are made for joy, why is life so full of pain?

JOY

What on the surface seems like a cosmic trap is really an opportunity. True joy can only be obtained through the acceptance of our heartache. We will never truly experience the ecstasy God has planted in our stories until we count the pain and loss that are also present. Pain is always embedded alongside the moments of freedom. Joy is forever bound to sorrow. True celebration will continually encompass feelings of loss and memories of loneliness. This is certainly true about becoming a father. Most of us men miss out on the joy that can await us in the early stages of fatherhood because we never stop and count the losses that becoming a dad brings into our lives.

1. Robert L. Dupont, *The Selfish Brain: Learning from Addiction* (Hazelden, Center City, MN: 1997).

As selfish and shallow as it might sound, besides sleep, one of the most tangible losses parenthood has brought to me (Stephen) is fewer opportunities to dine out. I love eating out. Nothing feels more celebratory than having dinner at a great restaurant with friends . . . fabulous conversation over a fantastic meal. But as a parent, with restraints on time, energy, and money, opportunities to eat out have been drastically reduced. To satisfy my desire for restaurants, we tried taking the babies along. But this proved difficult; in the process, I discovered that there are three developmental stages of eating out with children: (1) nursing/bottle feeding, (2) importing food, and (3) the children's menu.

Phase one, nursing/bottle-feeding, is, on the surface, most normal. Depending on what part of the country you live in and your wife's proclivity to bearing her breast (even partially) in public, breast-feeding while out and about may not be an option.

If your wife breast feeds as ours did, this means that the child always has a ready, steady supply of food. However, if your wife leans toward modesty, she may spend more time in the car or restroom than she does in the restaurant.

Phase two, importing food, is slightly more cumbersome. Preparing to go out to eat with a toddler in many ways resembles packing for an Everest expedition.

"Vegetables?"	*"Check."*
"Bag of Cheerios?"	*"Check."*
"Piece of fruit?"	*"Check."*
"Jar of fruit?"	*"Check."*
"Sippy cup of water?"	*"Check."*
"Sippy cup of juice?	*"Check."*
"Sippy cup of milk?"	*"Check."*
"Spoon?"	*"Check."*

"Bibs?"	*"Check."*
"Handy wipes?"	*"Check."*
"Diapers?"	*"Check."*
"Toys?"	*"Check."*

As you arrive at the restaurant, the car becomes your new base camp—a place to rest and retreat when the climate of being away from home becomes too difficult. It's also a place to stow your heavier, more cumbersome gear—like strollers, car seats, and play pens—as well as a shelter to fall back to for changing diapers and calling friends and family for support and encouragement.

Dining off of the children's menu is restricting. Grilled-cheese sandwiches, chicken finger baskets, and mac-n-cheese are staples of the children's menu. When your dining world is confined to only those eateries that serve kids' menus, your taste buds and waistline will suffer. And as my wife and I have discovered, not all grilled-cheese sandwiches are created equal.

This juvenile favorite is made in various ways, ranging from being truly grilled on an open flame with gourmet frommage (my favorite), to being cooked on the griddle with lots of butter, to being toasted like a panini, to being merely microwaved ("Yuck," as my daughter said). For recommendations, stick to privately owned restaurants and nicer hamburger joints. As far as fast-food chains go, Sonic is consistent, though the bread-to-cheese ratio is unbalanced. In a pinch, McDonald's will grill a hamburger bun with just cheese. Arby's has good bread, but ordering this sandwich off-menu makes the quality inconsistent. Regardless of what they say at Baha Fresh and Taco Bell, grilled-cheese quesadillas does not a sandwich make.

As you can tell, we have plenty of experience with grilled cheese. Well . . . so much for a thick pork chop braised in an apple glaze served with buttery, thick mashed potatoes and grilled vegetables.

Embracing Joy

Fatherhood calls us to acknowledge our heart and embrace the truth that lives within us all. Becoming a joy-filled father is about embracing the hope that relationships really can be good, full, and rich. It is about entering into and leading our children toward an abundant life replete with pain and mystery.

The priorities of joy-filled fathering must never be about doing more, learning more, or acquiring more skills. Rather, our focus as godly men must remain about discovering a life of authenticity and abundance based in the person of Christ. It is about stepping into the mystery of being and living truthfully out of how we are uniquely and wonderfully made. Learning and action must flow from this authenticity if it is to bring sanctification to ourselves and our families. As fathers, we are called to acknowledge and experience our own unique, divine createdness and likewise, experience and acknowledge the uniqueness of our children. This can only be done by naming, facing, and embracing our losses—the loss of free time, the loss of couplehood, the loss of money, the loss of privacy, the loss of sleep, the loss of freedom, the loss of quiet, to name only a few.

The more we know our children and our spouses, and the more we are known by them, the more we are alive to life. Without a doubt, we possess a hunger for intimacy, authenticity, and freedom that demands to be fed and is not easily satiated. We are profoundly relational, and we must participate in the experience of intimate and authentic relationship in order to live the abundant life for which we were made.

We can enter into the fathering experience having something different and unique to offer. We are capable of entering in with only half of our hearts present. We need not wait until we feel 100 percent enthusiasm and confirmation. If so, we could remain on the sidelines forever. It is revealing that we can feel so much love for our wives in some moments and can fantasize about leaving them in the same day. Dan Allender, in his book, *How Children Raise Parents*, speaks to this reality in saying that "marriage is the moist soil that grows both the weeds of sin and the roses of redemption. No other relationship requires more, gives so little and so much, and exposes both the best and the worst of our souls."[2] It is when we reach the point of experiencing a relationship that "gives so little" and exposes "the worst of our souls" that many decide to call it off.

So the question becomes, are you willing to step into mystery—boldly going where you haven't gone before? Are you courageous enough to step into uncharted territory and attempt to be present in it? Are you willing to be curious about something you don't really understand? Will you move beyond what is familiar and comfortable?

Are you as happy *as* she is? That word "as" is a funny word. It can mean equal to, but it can also mean "the same as" or "similar to." Are you happy *like* she is? Probably not, but we're not certain you need to be. For men and women to work off the same page, we don't have to be on the same line or even reading the same words. God made men and women differently. He made us in very unique ways and created us for unique purposes, and yet He designed us for relationship and parenting together. There's the mystery. He designed two different people to become one flesh.

2. Dan B. Allender, *How Children Raise Parents: The Art of Listening to Your Family* (WaterBrook Press, Colorado Springs, CO: 2003) p. 94.

Poop Patrol

Okay, men—get ready. Never before has it been so acceptable for you to engage in "potty talk". You and your wife will frequently be talking about and admiring your baby's prowess during the next several years. So, let's talk about poop.

Sometime in the first few days of life, your baby will have his or her first bowel movement, known as meconium. It is a thick, black, sticky substance that filled your baby's intestines during pregnancy. After it is eliminated, your baby will begin to have regular stools that differ in color and texture depending on your baby's diet. If your baby is breastfed, the stools should resemble light-colored mustard with seedlike particles. If formula-fed, your baby's stools will be tan or yellow in color and a bit firmer than a breastfed baby (no firmer than peanut butter). Some variations in color and consistency are normal.

When should you become concerned? If you notice that your baby has hard, dry stools or has frequent stools with an unusually high liquid content, something is not operating properly. In both cases, be sure that your baby is not dehydrated. If at any time you see large amounts of blood, mucus, or water in the stool, call your pediatrician immediately.

The frequency of stools varies widely. Some babies will poop after every feeding, while some older breastfed babies may have only one bowel movement a week. However, if your baby is formula-fed, he or she should have at least one bowel movement per day. Your baby should have at least four wet diapers per day. It may be helpful initially to post a chart by the changing table to keep track of what's happening in those dirty diapers. That way, you will not have to rely on your sleep-deprived mind to recount how many diapers you've changed throughout the day.

> "ADVENTURE, WITH ALL ITS REQUISITE DANGER AND WILDNESS, IS A DEEPLY SPIRITUAL LONGING WRITTEN INTO THE SOUL OF MAN."
>
> —JOHN ELDREDGE, *WILD AT HEART*

CHAPTER 3
Am I Ready?

A few months before my (Stephen) first child was born, I noticed that my pants were fitting more snuggly. I had to sit differently after lunch at work each day. A few weeks after that, I had to inhale deeply in order to button them in the morning. A month before my daughter was born, I had to go buy a bigger size. Enough is enough, I said. At my wife's next OBGYN appointment, I followed her back when she went to weigh in. After she weighed, I took a turn on the scale. It was one of those medical scales with the weight-and-balance. I moved the weight to the 150 notch and slid the counter-balance a few inches to the right toward 160. The rod didn't even begin to tilt. I nudged the counter-balance a few more inches. 170. Still no movement. I nudged it again. 175. 180. 185, and the bar begin to give, finally balancing at 187 1/2 pounds. "Holy Cow!" I exclaimed (except that I didn't really say, "Cow").

Heather looked at me with a knowing grin. With only four weeks left in her pregnancy, I had out-gained her in weight. By the time the baby would be born early the next month, I would have packed on thirty extra pounds. I had a serious case of what, in the South, we refer to as Dun-Lap Disease—meaning my stomach had dun lapped over my belt. In the anxiety of approaching fatherhood, I had turned to food (dessert in particular) to alleviate my fear. While the wandering Israelites may have bowed down to the golden calf, I fell at thrones of Duncan Hines and

Nabisco and Little Debbie and Sara Lee. All this eating kept my heart stuffed shut, so that the real questions were never allowed to surface. Obviously, I didn't feel ready, and I questioned my ability to be a father.

BEING PREPARED

Our cultural institution of American boyhood, the Boy Scouts, touts as its motto, "Be Prepared." The positive impact the BSA has made on our society is far too extensive to begin to mention. This is an entire organization ordered around the idea of training and equipping young men to engage the challenges of life with confidence. In adulthood, many of us spend years in a university or technical school in order to get ready for a chosen profession, only to realize that what we really needed to know in order to be successful we could only learn on the job. As men, we have a deep-seated need for feeling ready.

No place is that as true than when it hits the core of our masculinity: sex. Viagra was the most successful prescription drug ever launched in America. Projected U.S. sales for 2004 were around $919 million. A similar impotence drug, Cialis, the "weekend pill," guarantees up to thirty-six hours of effectiveness and generated $109 million in sales in its first nine months on the market. In 2004, Levitra was expected to bring in $174 million domestically. Prescription male sexual enhancement medication accounts for more than $1 billion in sales annually in the U.S. Any way you look at it, that's big business. A glimpse at these numbers tells us one thing for sure: Men want to feel ready.[1]

For his birthday one year, a friend of ours received fly-fishing lessons. Every week, he learned casting from Chuck, a noted master fisherman. Practicing daily in his backyard, our friend became skilled in a variety of different casts. He

1. M. Herper and A. Lagorce, "Monday Matchup, Viagra vs. Levitra." Forbes. com, accessed October 6, 2003.

soon invested in thousands of dollars of tackle: rod, reel, waders, shoes, vest, hat, line, and flies. He devoured book after book on his new avocation. As the spring approached, he planned his first trip to Montana for a week on the river.

The time finally came. His heart was full of anticipation and excitement. Once on the river, he waded out into the cold, hip-deep water and tied on his fly. As his arm found the rhythm of the casting motion he had practiced for weeks in the backyard, he saw a fish rise in a shallow pool on the other side of the stream. His heart began to pound as he let out more line, increasing the distance of his cast. The air was still except for the sound of his rod and line moving in time overhead.

Then . . . YANK!!! Surprised, he looked over his shoulder to find his line hopelessly entangled in the thick brush on the bank behind him. His only recourse was to cut his line and restring his entire reel. All his practice, preparation, and equipment had not readied him for the reality of being on the river. There were no riverbanks in his backyard.

Every week, we encounter men in our counseling offices—successful, brilliant, creative, wise men—who are confounded by their children and their role as a father. We have worked with influential businessmen who successfully manage hundreds of employees every day but tremble at the idea of looking their teenage son in the eye. We have wept with stoic patriarchs when they have had to bury a newborn. We have helped men who have chosen to be so physically absent from their families that their own children have trouble recognizing them. We have sat with brokenhearted and confused dads as they try to navigate the stormy waters with a pregnant adolescent daughter. At some point, all of these men in some way acknowledged that they were not ready for this.

We hope that as a dad, you will never have to encounter

any of the heartaches mentioned above. But sadly, reality tells us some of you will. And if not any of these, life will bring you its own wrinkle unique to your circumstance, situation, and story through the face of your children.

As men and fathers, we long to get it right, fix it, and be ready. Nevertheless, there is no class, book, or teaching that will alone prepare us for fatherhood. There is no boot camp that will get us ready for all that it takes to be a dad. As men, we desperately want to believe that a class on how to change diapers, make a bottle, and swaddle a baby is enough. It's not. We put our faith in principles and prescriptions in an effort to successfully raise a happy child. These fail. Our beliefs are false hopes fueled by a refusal to accept the complexity, confusion, and chaos of fatherhood.

MYSTERY VS. MASTERY

Masculinity is synonymous with engagement and movement. At the heart of every male lies a desire for exploration. This is most evident in children. At three, my (Stephen) firstborn would ask me to go on dark adventures in which we would turn out the lights and walk through the house with only a flashlight—unsure of what lay around the corner.

I (David) see this design in both of my sons, also. I have seen it from the earliest moments of their existence. When we spend time at a park, I enjoy standing back and watching their play. My boys love adventure. They want the tallest slide. One of my sons has yet to learn that you actually can slide down with your feet first. He strongly believes the only way to enjoy it is face-first. He laughs with delight and a sense of accomplishment when he tears down with his face to the wind. Every mulch pile is a mountain to climb. Every Lego tower is purposed for destruction. My sons crave adventure!

My wife gets a little sad and fearful as fall comes to a close and we prepare ourselves for winter in Tennessee. For the parents of young children, this translates into shorter days of light, colds, ear infections, and a desperate search for wide-open space that is warm. My sons need space to roam. They love the wild. Much of their behavior can be dictated by how long they have been confined to a small space.

This craving for adventure doesn't stop at childhood, though we may numb it so as to not recognize it. God has crafted the male heart with a penchant for preparation. Ironically, He has also designed us with a curiosity for the unseen, a deep desire for exploration, and a hunger for adventure. The reality of the masculine experience of full living is that the greater the adventure, the less we can prepare for it.

Human history is full of brave and curious men who have set off toward the horizon, putting the safety of the city at their backs, in an effort to fill their hunger for discovery and longing for glory. The Greeks and Vikings were famous in the ancient world for their heroing explorations. The Spanish and English pushed westward across the ocean to "discover" the Americas. The American soul uniquely embraces this spirit of the wild. Names like Lewis and Clark, Daniel Boone, Edward H. Harriman, and Neil Armstrong fill the annals of our nation's short history. The American psyche is shaped and anchored by the vision of the rugged frontier.

You don't have to sail the seas or journey to the moon to experience this quest for discovery. All you have to do is open the eyes of your heart to the full experience of being present in your own home. Take the first step into the unexplored places you find yourself unsure.

The idea of completing a task and checking it off my (David) list entices me. I particularly love this sense of accomplishment when things around me are chaotic. While in graduate school, I organized my tools and belongings in the garage seven times while attempting to study for my comprehensive exams. When preparing for the arrival of my twin sons, we bought, sold, and renovated a house. The idea of mastery is not limited to me. It pervades our culture. This is evidenced in the many self-help books that promise a select number of habits for success in work, marriage, parenting, investing, and relationships. We long to believe that success can be experienced if only we master seven habits. I wish it were that simple. I long for it to be.

When it comes to fathering, we crave mastery; however, the art of fathering was never intended to be mastered. It never will be. It was established to bring about uncertainty, joy, confusion, celebration, fear, and hope. It is designed to expose us at the core of who we are as men. Through fathering, we become more connected with our deficits and dependence. Here's the deep blessing of having children: You will have the chance to find out you are not enough.

Is any part of you asking, "Where is the blessing in that? Connecting with my incapacity doesn't feel like much of a blessing." It's part of what Christ meant in His teaching when He said,

> "Blessed are the poor in spirit,
> for theirs is the kingdom of heaven.
> Blessed are those who mourn,
> for they will be comforted.
> Blessed are the meek,
> for they shall inherit the earth.
> Blessed are those who hunger and thirst for
> righteousness, for they will be filled."
> (Matt. 5:3-6)

We will receive blessing in experiencing brokenness, sadness, and uncertainty. The journey of pregnancy and parenting will take us to these places. Adam and Eve, the first parents, must have experienced all of these things in their journey. In the fourth chapter of Genesis, we are told of the birth of three sons to this couple and the loss of one. This chapter gives testimony to the first experience of parenting and closes with these words: "At that time men began to call on the name of the LORD" (Gen. 4:26).

It was the experience of parenting that brought them to a place of calling on God. Nothing else had taken them there yet. Not their fear, not their shame, not their guilt, not their loneliness. Doesn't that speak to what is required of us in fathering? Doesn't that speak to the mystery and the uncertainty? "At that time men began to call on the name of the LORD."

Get Ready to Fail

There are two photographs in my (David) office that I can see from where I sit the majority of the day. One is a photograph of seven scruffy men in front of a wide lake. It is a trip that I took years ago with six men who I love and who have played a significant role in my life. The other is a photograph of me standing on a dock in the Bahamas. I am holding a twenty-eight-pound mahi mahi that I caught on a deep-sea fishing trip with some friends back in the late nineties. Both pictures remind me that adventure and wildness are longings of mine. When experienced, they stir passion and bring pleasure. I keep these photographs near to remind me of what I desire, who I am, and how I was designed.

The photograph of the dolphin has a revealing story behind it. It was a trip to Marsh Harbour in 1999 with my wife and some dear friends. We stayed on a boat for the week and would daily set out for different islands in the Bahamas to hike/explore, sightsee, eat, and fish. The first day of fishing, I nailed that twenty-eight-pound dolphin. After a long, vigorous battle, I reeled him in to shouts of delight. He would be the catch of my lifetime (so far). I remember the first bite of him—seasoned and grilled to perfection. It was pure glory. The following day, we set out for Guana and did some bottom fishing. I caught seventeen strawberry grouper and yellow tail snapper in a short span of time. I remember thinking it couldn't get any better than this moment—the company of people I love and enjoy, a perfect day on the water, and the satisfaction of a big catch.

The first part of the trip back to the dock, I reveled in the moment and drank in the sunshine and the smell of the ocean as I glanced at my bounty in the cooler, just waiting to be grilled and enjoyed. And then the tide turned. I remember a slight unsettled feeling in my stomach. I looked out over the wake behind the boat and noticed the waves seemed a bit rougher.

Little by little, moment by moment, I began to feel more uneasy and nauseated. The feeling would intensify over the next minutes, and the ride home began to seem like hours and days. I tried desperately to get settled, but nothing helped . . . nothing but throwing up everything I had enjoyed that day and the glorious day before. And then I threw up what I had eaten the week before and then the months before. Lastly, I threw up the internal organs that I wasn't really using.

It was a long, tumultuous, "take-me-out-of-my-misery" kind of trip back. I thought we would never arrive. It took me hours to feel normal again. Even standing still on dry land, I felt the movement of crashing waves. While I so desperately wanted to revel in the glory of my day and to savor my catch, I settled for ginger ale and called it a day. I went from a glimpse of heaven to a nightmare in a matter of minutes. I moved from serenity to disaster at the strike of a wave. Such is the story of my life . . . triumph and tragedy, glory and chaos.

I am reminded of a scene in the film, *The Count of Monte Cristo*. The story is one of betrayal, adventure, redemption, and revenge. In one particular scene, the Count is giving a toast at the birthday celebration of Albert Mondego, a young man he encounters in Rome. It is also a ceremony of this boy's coming into manhood. In his toast, he admonishes Albert with these words: "Life is a storm, my young friend. You will bask in the sunlight one moment, be shattered on the rocks the next. What makes you a man . . . is what you do when that storm comes.

Biblical historians tell us that ancient Jewish culture looked at male development in stages. Childhood (birth to age twelve) was a time of innocence. Around thirteen, males were considered adults in that they were held accountable for keeping the law. However, these "men" were not expected to exhibit the full weight of wisdom until they turned thirty years old. The core of this thinking acknowledges the idea that with age comes some wisdom. But the reality is, however old you are, twenty-five, fifty-five, or ninety-five, you are not fully equipped to be a parent. You will never really be ready.

For sure, you have many questions about what it means to be a good enough parent. If not, it is doubtful that you would be reading this book. The secret to being a great father is being willing to learn from your children. Successful parenting has a lot to do with learning how to handle failure—both yours and your child's.

The truth is that it is okay to feel ill prepared. Nothing to date has expressly prepared you for parenting. Certainly, you have had many experiences in life that have given you a glimpse of being a dad, but there is no major in college entitled "Bachelor of Fatherhood." At the same time, be comforted in the fact that God has authored your entire story to come to this point. This is a season that God has set aside for you to grow in wisdom and influence. It is your responsibility and opportunity to turn toward the moment with your whole heart, as best as you are able. Bring all your fear, joy, vision, doubt, hope, dreams, and longings into focus and take the leap.

A Royal Coronation

Whether we are aware of it or not, this new experience of fatherhood will reshape our story. If we let it, it will inform both our past and our future, giving us greater understanding and appreciation of many things. Early fatherhood can be a time of personal transformation. If we are willing, becoming a dad will simultaneously awaken our pasts and thrust us toward our futures. It is a time of remembering and dreaming. It's a season where the soil of the heart is turned over and prepared to grow and renew life.

One way this happens is that fatherhood affords men the opportunity to move from being a prince to being a king. It is a time of accepting the weighty mantle of authority. When you become a father, you are endowed with additional power and influence. You will be able to bless another person's life like no one else. And with the power to bless comes also the responsibility to do so. As a king, you have the privilege, opportunity, and obligation to uncover the image of God latent in your child.

We aren't designed to feel "ready" to become fathers. Culture would have us believe we can be. You will find plenty of other books written for expectant and new fathers full of lists of things to do and not to do. This book also contains lists. We hope those lists are helpful. We've read other books that proved to be helpful as well. However, there is no mastery. We'd love to recommend ten habits of perfect parenting to you, but they are only habits recommended in the midst of mystery. We want to give you permission to not feel ready. Later in this book, you will encounter a chapter titled "How Do I Prepare?" Our hope is that it will offer you some strong ideas around preparing for this adventure. Heads up! All of it is centered around preparing for mystery. Do you have the courage to step into the mystery? The ride is wild and unpredictable. You read the caution signs on the way into the ride. You have some idea about what to expect and no idea at all.

Welcome to the mystery.

DATING YOUR WIFE

Parenting definitely takes a lot out of you. If you aren't careful to continue pursuing your wife, your marriage will suffer. How can you ensure that you remain connected and engaged?—with one-on-one time together. Here are some tips for making it happen:

• Caring for a newborn is exhausting. Your wife may need a nap and some time to recharge before she has much to give you.

• Plan a date, and with your wife's assistance, arrange childcare. We suggest writing out instructions for the babysitter about your child's schedule, needs, etc.

• Give your wife some time off before your date. Come home early and take over for her so that she has time to get ready and anticipate the evening together.

• If you are unable to find a babysitter or your budget doesn't allow one, consider baby-sitting swaps with friends or create a date at home. You could cook dinner for your wife (make sure to prepare something that reheats easily in case the baby cries), rent a movie, play a game, or do anything else you would enjoy together.

• Figure out what best communicates love to your wife. Is it time with you, affection, cleaning a messy kitchen? Remember that it is probably different than how you would like your wife to love you. Figure it out, and then show your love often.

• Other date ideas: taking a walk in the park, going out to dinner, seeing a movie, listening to music, attending a sporting event, cooking together, taking a class together, reading to her, going to the theater, exercising or playing a sport together, hiking, picnicking, running errands, dancing, etc.

Sex Pre- and Post-Baby

Pre-Baby

She is exhausted, nauseated, uncomfortable, growing, etc. You are stressed, anxious, and uptight. She may not even be interested in sex during parts of her pregnancy. If you do wind up in the mood at the same time, you will realize that sex gets more challenging as your wife's tummy grows. You will have to get creative and vary your positions. By the end of the pregnancy, be prepared for a drastic increase in sexual activity. A widely held belief that sex can trigger labor seems to get most women very interested in sex. (Don't worry about hurting the baby during intercourse. Doctors agree that if your pregnancy is normal, there is no danger to the fetus).

Post-Baby

The majority of women are given permission to resume normal sexual activity at the six-week postpartum appointment. Try to refrain from comments like, "But it's been six weeks." You saw what happened to your wife's body during delivery, and she may be in pain. Wouldn't you be? She will need you to be slow and gentle and use a personal lubricant generously. Your best tools are understanding and patience!

If your wife is nursing, you may get a chance to sample your baby's diet. Frequently sex will stimulate your wife's milk letdown reflex. It's possible that this could take place during your experience of intimacy.

As with every aspect of marriage, communication is critical. If you are able to communicate about your sex life, chances are that both your emotional and physical intimacy will deepen.

"SOME PEOPLE SKIP THROUGH LIFE;
SOME PEOPLE ARE DRAGGED THROUGH IT."

—DONALD MILLER, *BLUE LIKE JAZZ*

CHAPTER 4
Is This Really Happening?

February 2004 will go down in history as one of the worst months in the life of the Thomas family. While we can laugh as we look back on it now, there was no laughter then. It all began in December 2003 when I (David) realized I had mistakenly committed to teach two classes, both beginning in February. It was an error on my part that wouldn't be monumental in itself, but, mixed with other obligations, would make my load too heavy. And when my load is too heavy, my wife ends up carrying more than her fair share of responsibility. In addition to teaching, I had also scheduled to take my licensure exam the second week of February. Stephen and I had set a personal deadline to finish a publishing proposal around the same time, and I was carrying a full load of clients with a four-week wait list.

We struggled through January trying to prepare ourselves in advance as best we could. I was working throughout the week, writing late at night and on weekends, and studying for the exam in any spare moment I could find. I was feeling the weight of not being in the kids' lives and not caring well for my wife. If January felt this bad, how would we survive the month of February?

It came, as we knew it would, and I kicked off each of the courses with some level of clarity and creativity. Two days after the second course had begun, my wife called me at work to inform me that one of my sons had started with what seemed to be a stomach virus. We set a strategy for how to best care for him and quarantine me in light of the teaching commitment and the licensure exam in less than five days. I came home that evening to piles of laundry covered in throw up and four battle worn soldiers in my home. As is usually the case with any virus or infection, it takes approximately twenty-four to thirty-six hours to pass from one child in my home to the next. This time it took about thirty-six hours, and the boys began to harmonize in their wailing and vomiting. My wife would change sheets approximately eight to ten times a day (as fast as she could wash them). I walked about the house fumigating with disinfectant and hoping for the best. I made it through another class and three more days of work and crammed through Friday for the test.

I went to bed that evening at 9:30 p.m. in hopes of a long rest before my four-hour exam on Saturday. I woke around 3:15 a.m. and needed to go to the bathroom. I felt a bit unsettled, but chalked it up to anxiety before the big test. I went back to bed, only to return to the bathroom thirty minutes later. I wasn't throwing up, but I was losing everything in the other direction.

It was obvious that I wasn't going back to sleep anytime soon, so I threw in the towel and headed for the den to do some more studying. After all, I was awake, and I might as well study. I continued to cram and make periodic trips to the bathroom. I eventually showered and headed out early to get to the exam site on time.

I arrived at the test site, signed in, and barely made it to the bathroom before I threw up everywhere. I thought to myself, *This is not happening to me!* I went back in to speak with the proctor. I informed her that I believed my sons had given me the stomach virus, and I needed to know what was involved in getting exempt from the test. She informed me that I'd need a note from my doctor. I would then have to send that note with a letter to the appeal board requesting exemption, but that did not guarantee it . . . or a refund for my very costly test fee. I informed her that my doctor didn't keep office hours on Saturday. She recommended that I go to the emergency room. I envisioned myself there in the snow for six to seven hours vomiting in a bed pan until I could be seen by a resident, who would write me a note that the appeal board would throw away and then go to lunch at an expensive restaurant with my test money.

I decided to gamble and take the stupid test. After all, you do feel better for about twenty minutes after you throw up, until the cycle starts again. The proctor assured me I could sign out to go to the restroom as many times as I wanted. I proceeded to do so every thirty minutes for the next four hours. I would throw up, come back and answer twenty-five to twenty-eight questions, and then do it all over again. It would be the longest four hours of my life.

I somehow answered every question and hit the return button on the computerized test. They asked me to evaluate the test site and test experience while I waited for the computer to tally my score. It was a bad time to ask for feedback! However, I did, and just as I finished, my results were displayed:

Passing Score: 75
Your Score: 74

I considered vomiting on the screen and the proctor on my way out the door, but I chose the snow instead. I drove home and threw up twice on the way. I entered the house and was greeted by my tired wife and two dehydrated toddlers, and just as I rounded the corned to fall into my bed, my daughter threw up for the first time in the hallway. It was like something out of a National Lampoon vacation movie. The look on Connie's face was one of "take me far away from here." I collapsed into the bed and announced my defeat. She was unaware that I had awoken early and started the stomach virus on test morning. She would now nurse four people back to health.

We laugh now as we remember this story and that awful month. The classes are done; the proposal was submitted and evolved into the book you are now reading. I will someday take the licensure exam again. Everyone in my family is healthy, and we lived to survive the stomach plague of Winter 2004. We laugh now, but no one was laughing then . . . only crying and puking.

My capacity to give and to have insight in those moments is fairly limited. Although I knew that virus would likely run its course in forty-eight hours, I wanted to be taken out in the midst of it. I remember thinking, *February is the shortest month of the year, and this is the longest twenty-eight days of my life.*

Do you remember the longest month of your life? Can you recall any of the chaos surrounding that month? Was it a project at work? Was it tension or conflict involving your wife? Did the month stretch into a season? Did the seasons blend into a year? Where did you go with the chaos?

Let's look at the first scene involving chaos:

> In the beginning God created the heavens and the earth. Now the earth was formless and empty, darkness was over the surface of the deep, and the Spirit of God was hovering over the waters. And God said, "Let there be light," and there was light. God saw that the light was good, and he separated the light from the darkness. God called the light "day," and the darkness he called "night." And there was evening, and there was morning–the first day. (Gen. 1:1-5)

In the beginning, there was empty, formless darkness. It was chaotic. What was God doing in the midst of this darkness? We are told in verse two that He was hovering. From the beginning, we know that there was chaos and God was present. What did He do next? In verse three, we learn that He spoke into the chaos. In the following passages, He brings beauty, order, and life. And we are made in His image.

Our good friend, Al Andrews, coauthored an amazing book years ago, with Don Hudson and Larry Crabb, entitled *The Silence of Adam*, that speaks specifically to men moving into a world of chaos. In this book, they pose the question, "Could it be that God intended for men to behave like him by courageously moving into whatever spheres of mystery they encounter and speaking with imagination and life-giving power into the confusion they face?"

I have the capacity to move into chaos to provide beauty and order. That doesn't mean our purpose is to straighten all things out. It simply means our presence has great purpose.

God intends for us to follow His lead. We are built to speak words of life. Our presence has purpose, and we are called to move with intention. We are also called to be present in the midst of chaos. There will be many Februarys in life. We cannot escape that reality.

The process of fathering will always involve chaos and tension. The experience of fathering is designed to be both productive and destructive. And we are called to be right in the middle of the tears, the excitement, the tragedy, and the triumph, the laughter and the regurgitation, the joy and the sorrow. We are made for it all. We are equipped for the chaos.

In the film *Nine Months*, Sam Faulkner (Hugh Grant) has it all: a beautiful girlfriend, a successful career, and a brand-new, red Porsche convertible. But his life changes when his girlfriend, Rebecca Taylor (Julianne Moore), tells him she is pregnant while on a picturesque drive through the Napa Valley. Sam, a child psychologist, is driving and lamenting a recent patient at work, while Rebecca is earnestly studying her checkbook calendar, counting days since her last menstrual cycle.

Sam: I don't know about Truman. I'll get him to open up, but he's got very severe problems, and we know who we can thank for those problems, don't we? You know. His parents.

Rebecca: Thirty-two.

Sam: It's incredible. The state requires that you take a written test to drive a car, but any complete moron can become a parent and destroy a child's life. It's like people just have babies on a whim.

Rebecca: Thirty-four.

Sam: Surely, to be a parent you have to plan ahead.

Rebecca: Thirty-six.

Sam: Say to yourself, "Do I really want to become a parent?"

Rebecca: Thirty-eight.

Sam: "Am I ready for that responsibility?"

Rebecca: I'm pregnant.

Sam: What? Pregnant?

Rebecca: Watch out! Watch out! Ah! Watch out!

The camera cuts to an on-rushing tractor trailer. (In his shock Sam has crossed the center lane of traffic.) Sam swerves to miss it and drives off the road through a construction site and crashes headfirst into a parked bulldozer—wrecking his Porsche.

Rebecca: Well, I guess you don't want the baby.

A few scenes later, we see Sam pulling up to the dance school where Rebecca works. He is having a conversation with himself as he makes his way to the classroom where she is teaching.

Sam: I can't be a father. I can't. I ca . . . I . . . Why would I want to have a child? Just so he can call me a b------ in ten years' time? We'd have to move out. We don't have space for a child. Rebecca and me, we're wonderful together. It's just insane to spoil it. Just the two of us that's how it should be. This baby is not a good idea.

He pauses outside her classroom.

    That's what I'll tell her.

He calls to her, and she approaches.

    I'll tell her now.

Rebecca: Hi.

Sam: Beck.

They embrace and greet each other. After their conversation, he doesn't say a word.

Like Sam, when we discover ourselves on the threshold of fatherhood, our reaction may be disbelief to the point of incapacitation. Unsure of the reality of the moment, we ask ourselves, "Is this really happening?" This question is common as we enter fatherhood; however, its origins and meaning are very specific to each man.

A Specific Question

For some, the question, "Is this really happening?" comes from a position of gratitude. The question serves as a declaration of joy, "I can't believe how good this is." Others find this question a statement of awe, exposing their humility in the grand scheme of life. For these men, "Is this really happening?" may mean, "I don't know what to do. This is so much bigger than me." For still others, "Is the really happening?" is a refusal to accept their position in life. It's a fight against their lot that says, "I'm not ready. There are things I need to accomplish first."

For most of us, however, wrapped in this question of doubt is a menagerie of unspoken experiences and expectations. For Sam, this question comes from a place of dread, being needed by others, and resistance to the finality of commitment. Even though very much in love with his girlfriend, he is profoundly self-centered and incapable of knowing others beyond how they meet his needs. For Sam, the question, "Is this really happening?" is a statement of un-surrendered fear of losing the predictability of his life.

I (Stephen) remember asking this question when Heather went into labor with our first child. It was Sunday afternoon, and I was coaching a soccer game thirty miles from home. She called me on my cell phone with only a few minutes left in the game to tell me she was having contractions. "Don't rush. It could be hours before we need to go to the hospital," she said. The whistle blew. I gave my team instructions for their next game and then jogged to my car, jumped in, and headed toward home.

The only direct route from the fields to where we lived was via a two-lane country highway. I remember thinking to myself as I pulled out of the soccer complex, *I have a legitimate excuse to drive as fast as I want.* I darted off, racing like Mario Andretti, swerving around slower traffic, and dodging back into my lane. At some point, I had the notion that putting on my hazard lights would justify my ludicrous driving.

On the way home, I called Heather a few times, but she didn't answer, and I began to worry. Had she already gone to the hospital? Was she okay?

I screeched into the driveway. Heather's father was standing on the porch. A million fears raced through my head. Then I noticed Heather up the street casually waking the dog with her mother. Heather's dad was smiling.

I hopped out of the car and waited for her on the sidewalk, my heart frantic with indecision and expectation. As she approached, I moved toward her thinking to myself, *Is this real? Am I really about to be a father?* I had no picture in my mind of how gloriously rewarding fatherhood could be. As I stood there watching Heather move toward me, I was lost in my own joy, fear, anticipation, and lack of vision about what was about to happen.

Do you know the foundation of your disbelief? Do you know from where this question arises in your own heart? By addressing this question and its origins, you can gain insight, awareness, and understanding of your story, and you can get a glimpse of how you are uniquely made as a man and as a father. You will also discover that "Is this really happening?" may mean different things for you at different times. Early in pregnancy, it may mean one thing. During labor and delivery, it may mean something else. And the first few weeks and months of your child's life, it will probably mean something altogether different.

DENIAL

Fatherhood is ripe with tension and chaos, but sometimes it is easier to deal with the stress of change by pretending that it's not real or ignoring its significance and/or risk. Or culture is full of metaphors for this strategy, such as, "whistling past the graveyard" and "sticking your head in the sand." Psychologists call this coping mechanism "denial." In reality, this is like trying to stop a tidal wave with an umbrella. No matter how much you try to avoid the effects of becoming a father, they will catch you—not that becoming a dad is like being hit by a tidal wave. (Who are we kidding? Yes it is.) If you choose to ignore the significance of this life event, you will miss the blessings God has set aside for us in this unique season.

Denial is understandable. Fatherhood is neither predictable nor practical. Asking the question, "Is this really happening?" is a way of pulling your head out of the sand and plugging your heart back into the flow of life. To not address this question leaves you disconnected and ineffectual. But to ask it is the beginning of living intentionally.

In *The Longing for Home*, Frederick Buechner writes, "In our lives in the world, the temptation is to always go where the world takes us, to drift with whatever current happens to be running strongest."[1] Asking the question, "Is this really happening?" calls us into the present because the only answer that is true is, "Yes!" And the reality is that whatever "this" represents for you is so much bigger than you could ever know.

Ignorance is Bliss

There is a marked difference between ignoring your heart and simply not knowing. When we became fathers for the first time, we both were ignorant. We didn't know what to do. We didn't know how to care for our wives. We were clueless.

My wife and I (Stephen) were looking at family movies a while back and stumbled across the one of us giving our daughter her first bath. We had no idea what we were

1. Frederick Buechner, *The Longing for Home: Recollections and Reflections* (HarperCollins, San Francisco, CA: 1996) p. 109.

doing. Babies don't come with instruction manuals (but fortunately, one of the books we had bought did).

Heather and I filled the kitchen sink with warm water and propped the book in a cookbook stand. We laid out two thick cotton bath towels on the counter and placed Emma Claire on them. We followed the instructions step by step. "Starting with your infant's head wipe gently with a towel and rinse with clean warm water." We nervously worked our way down her body, carefully cleaning every inch, until, a half an hour later, her pink newborn body sparkled.

The contrast with our son (our second child) could not be more striking. It's not that we loved him less or were less amazed by his presence in our family, we just knew more. We had learned that newborns don't do that much to get dirty. (They basically lay around all day and eat, sleep, and poop.) We knew whatever overlooked, dried gunk hidden in his neck folds we would surely get tomorrow or the day after.

That first bath with my daughter is a sacred memory. It is a moment that I will never forget: her sweet smell, the softness of her skin, her fight to stay awake, the look of confusion in her eyes. It was a perfect moment packed with innocence and naiveté (on all of our parts). It was an experience I was not afforded with my second child. Looking back, one lesson I've taken from the contrast of those events is that being goofy and incompetent is unavoidable, but if I show up and engage my heart, those moments can be extraordinary.

AUTHENTICITY, INTEGRITY, AND INTENTIONALITY

Authentic fatherhood is about showing up with all that you have and with all that you are (especially when you feel awkward or ill-prepared or insecure). Parenting with integrity means standing toe to toe with the conflict and chaos of relationships. An intentional father embraces opportunities that expose his vulnerability and intimacy— even if he doesn't know what he is doing. By moving into fatherhood with a commitment to authenticity, integrity, and intentionality, you have the opportunity to become more than you currently are.

Chip Dodd, in his book, *The Voice of the Heart*, describes this way of being more practically. Dodd instructs that in order to live fully, we must do three things: "feel our feelings, tell the truth, and give it to God." To elaborate, genuine passion-filled fatherhood means having an authentic experience of the heart—feeling your feelings. It is saying, "Yes!" to the emotion-wrapped desires and longings lying dormant in the soil of the masculine soul. Second, it is imperative that you share those inward experiences with those who matter most to you. This takes an intentional and rigorous commitment to honesty. For example, does your wife know what frightens you most about being a dad? Does she know what loneliness and unhealed hurts you carry from your own childhood? Are you aware of how your story lives itself out in your life?

Once your desires erupt from your heart and are exposed to others, you realize that you have very little power to fulfill these on your own. You are then faced with the very personal question, "Is God good enough and big enough to handle me?" If we answer this question with a "yes," then life becomes unpredictable and wild—in other words, free. If in our living, we reflect a "no," life will become habitual. We unplug our hearts. Christian thinker and writer Donald Miller warns of this in *Blue Like Jazz*: "I believe that the greatest trick of the devil is not to get us into some sort of evil but rather have us wasting time. This is why the devil tries so hard to get Christians to be religious. If he can sink a man's mind into habit, he will prevent his heart from engaging God."

What is keeping you from experiencing the Good News? What is holding you back from considering all that being a dad might have in store for you? What desires for yourself, your wife, and your child are you keeping hidden?

Marriage and Parenthood

The relationship that is impacted more than any other as fatherhood dawns on your life is the one you have with your spouse. Once a man and woman join with each other in the act of creating life, the terrain between them will never be the same. Their relationship becomes intertwined and tangled with the brambles and thickets of being a parent. Marriage and parenthood are two sides of the same coin.

Our ability to father is directly linked to our capacity as a husband. Similarly, our wives only mother as much as they join with us in marriage. The effect of these two preceding statements cannot be escaped: When the foundation of a marriage is unstable, the results will always be traumatic for the children. Your ability to parent comes directly from the quality of your marriage.

The best thing we can do for our children is not work on being a better "dad." In order to succeed as fathers, we must view the relationships with our children through the lens of marriage. Focusing on our children to the exclusion or alienation of our spouse is detrimental to their hope for a satisfying life. The most effective thing we as men can do as parents is commit to growing and maturing as husbands. You can never be a successful father unless you are first a successful husband.

One of God's primary plans for marriage is for the development of the family—making babies. This is seen clearly in Gen. 1:26-28, in which the cultural mandate is to fill and multiply. Obviously multiplication, at least in that context, is making babies. Historically, we see that marriage provides the best context for the heart of a child. But conversely, from God's point of view, the very purpose of parenting has less to do with the childbearing and more to do with growing each parent to be more like God.

Very simply, God is not that committed to making you, your marriage, or your family happy. (If that's His goal, He's doing a lousy job in the lives of many very faith-filled and devoted people.) To say God is unconcerned with our happiness is absurd. However, at a foundational level, God's commitment is to grow our holiness and not fundamentally to assure our happiness. In fact, God readily sacrifices our happiness in order to offer us opportunities for greater intimacy with Him, our spouses, and our children.

I (Stephen) mentioned in the last chapter that my son's birth was violent. Let me share more now. When Heather went into labor around midnight, our midwife, Valerie, suggested that Heather and I try to get some rest. We all expected a long day ahead, and we wanted to be as rested as possible. Heather and I lay there like two children on Christmas Eve, our hearts bursting with excitement and anticipation. As we lay there together, the mood mellowed as Heather was hit with a series of very strong contractions. After the contractions subsided a bit, I called the midwife to let her know we were coming in. I then called Heather's parents to come stay with our daughter so that we could leave for the birth center.

When Heather's parents arrived, I gathered our stuff, but before leaving, we all circled together to pray. Now I don't typically advocate long prayers, and this night was no exception. What was different was that I prayed for something very specific.

"Father God, I am so thankful. We can't wait to meet our new child. I am so grateful for what You are doing in our lives. Meet us in this process. Lord, let this birth tell Your story so that we have a chance to better know You. I don't necessarily pray that this be simple or easy (although that would be nice), but Father, let this be a time where we can experience You and see Your face. In Jesus' name I pray, amen."

As I ended my prayer, Heather and I made eye contact. She wore a question on her face; it was probably the same question I was asking myself—"What did I just say? Wait, God . . . I take it back." I knew enough to know God is most often revealed in moments of heartache.

We arrived at the birth center and were greeted by Valerie, who took us to a candlelit birthing suite. After moments of normalcy, Heather began massive contractions that didn't let up. Instead of coming in waves, they increased in strength over the next several minutes. Valerie suggested that Heather labor for a while in the tub. Heather complied.

Not long after getting in the tub (maybe half an hour), Heather said, "Valerie, I need to push." Within a few moments, the baby's head had crowned. Heather was in what seemed to me to be horrible pain. But she was making great progress. We were about to have a baby. I reached down into the water with a nervous hand and touched our baby's head.

Then another contraction and another push, but this time, the baby didn't move. Valerie's face changed, and her brow narrowed. "Heather. If the baby doesn't come out on this next push, I want you to get out of the tub," Valerie said sternly. And then added, "Do you understand?" underlining her previous sentence. And with only those three words, the pretense of control left the room, and my heart raced with fear.

Heather said, "Yes." And with the next contraction, Heather ferociously groaned as she pushed with everything in her soul. To no avail. The baby didn't budge.

And then everything slowed down. I helped Heather move from the tub as Valerie calmly, confidently, and yet emphatically gave instructions. "Heather. Get down on your hands and knees."

"Right here?" Heather asked, not so much in disbelief, but in seeking confirmation.

"Yes," Valerie said, nodding to the floor.

As Heather moved from the tub, I gaped at the head of my partially born child hanging from my wife's torso, its face blue and lifeless, like some kind of chubby doll.

The room was thick with birth's odor. Blood, sweat, and water dripped from Heather's exhausted body. Heather was prone on the floor with Valerie's hands around the baby's head. I stood over them—my head swimming with adrenaline and my heart faint with fear.

Valerie instructed Heather to turn onto her back. She did, and then I noticed that Valerie hands and wrists and forearms had disappeared into my wife's agonized body. Heather was pushing with all the force and courage that remained in her. Heather's mom, who rode with us to the center, was instructed to call the ambulance.

Lost and hopeless, I struggled for presence. "Valerie, what can I do?" I asked, almost begging for a purpose in the moment.

"Nothing," she responded. Then in almost the same breath, she said, "Pray. You can pray."

With that instruction, hope rushed in.

Heather was desperately calling, "Oh Jesus! Oh Jesus! We trust You. We trust You."

"Lord! . . . God! . . . Father! . . . Please help us," were the only words I could manage. I felt awkward and embarrassed, and my heart was flooded with questions. "Is my child dead? Is this it—is this how God is writing my story? Are Heather and I able to walk through this together? Can our marriage bear this kind of loss? How will we explain to our daughter that her baby brother or sister wouldn't be coming home?"

There was nothing I could do. Then I was struck with clarity and lightness. I felt it and knew it at the same time. I said to myself, "I am in the presence of God." That birthing suite had become the Holy of Holies. Amidst the stench and turmoil of birth mingled the glory of God. That moment, filled with terror and pain and powerlessness, was the most intimate I had ever been with my God. My heart sank into rest. Whether my child lived or died, somehow, it was well with my soul. God was the author of this story, not me. He was in charge, not me. When so much of me wanted to rage against the injustice of the moment, even more of me was abandoned to a peace that I to this day do not understand. This peace did not relieve or remove me from the confusion of the moment, but it did take the burden of the moment from my hands. I was certain that whatever the outcome was to be, it was God's responsibility. It was all so clear, and I was so thankful to be there with Heather . . . and with God.

All this happened in an instant. Our prayers. God's presence. And the birth of our son. He was delivered into this world blue and bloody and almost lifeless. He was not breathing and had only a faint heartbeat. Valerie worked to resuscitate him. I knelt down beside Heather, holding her naked and exhausted body in a pool of blood and water and fluids on the floor. We watched Valerie as she breathed life into our son.

"What's his name?" she asked. All we had settled on was a middle name, the name our fathers share. "Thomas." I replied. He began to breathe. His heartbeat gradually grew stronger over the next several hours. His face was swollen with purple bruises from the trauma of his journey into life. It would be hours before he could open one eye, then the other. It would be the next day before we named him.

After much thought, Heather and I named him Elijah (which means, "The Lord is God"). Elijah Thomas James was born 10 lb., 4 oz. and 23" long. That's big as babies come—even bigger when you consider my petite 5'4" wife. He is extraordinarily healthy today. A bit stubborn, willful, adventurous, but healthy.

I do not believe that if I had remained silent, God would have taken my son's life. For me, that is vain and narcissistic. I am not foolish enough to believe that I bear that kind of power. However, by crying out to Him, I had to come to terms with the reality that God is the author of my story, and I am powerless to so much of life.

God was willing to let my son rest between life and death in order to have me more dependent on and in relationship with Him. He was willing to break my heart in order to draw me closer to Him. This was not a test that I was to pass or fail, but rather an opportunity to meet Him in the chaos of life with all of my heart. His showing up was not (and is never) dependent on my participation.

Some months later, I heard this line in a song that helped me understand this even more clearly:

> *Maybe where the heart breaks in two,*
> *That's the only place Grace can break*
> *through*
> *to find you.*
> —David Wilcox, "Stronger Than Ever Now"

This heartbreak and brokenness create opportunities for us to be present, and presence is the essence of fatherhood.

"**O, BEWARE, MY LORD, OF JEALOUSY!** **IT IS THE GREEN-EYED MONSTER, WHICH DOTH MOCK THE MEAT IT FEEDS ON.**"

— *OTHELLO*,
WILLIAM SHAKESPEARE

CHAPTER 5
WHAT IF MY WIFE LOVES THE BABY MORE THAN ME?

When babies come home, everything changes. Sleep is reduced from a reasonable seven to nine hours a night to a scant three or four. Money previously spent on movies, ball games, and weekend trips is used to purchase diapers, baby food, and plastic toys. The sterile odor of childlessness is replaced by the perfume of soiled diapers, spit-up, and Johnson's Baby Shampoo. ESPN's *SportsCenter* is supplanted by *Sesame Street*.

This disruption is miniscule compared to what changes take place in marriage. All of the sudden, your relationship is wearing its clothes inside-out. Everything still fits, but the seams are exposed, and the lettering on your shirt is reversed. Your marriage is disoriented and radically different, but not wholly unfamiliar. You recognize your wife, as she does you, but the focus of your relationship has been adjusted—widened to include more of the landscape of life.

In the first few weeks and months following childbirth, couples have to relearn each other. Many things have changed, and we must work to redefine our relationships with our wives. One place this altered state of marriage is played out is in the arena of sex. Even if we get past the obstacles of fatigue, stress, and confusion, we must contend with the reality that our wives now share their bodies and hearts and minds with someone else.

....

Her focus is turned elsewhere. Many of her dreams about this moment are fulfilled, and unless there were medical or biological complications, she is focused on this new life (and therefore not you). The energy of her heart has been redirected from being a "couple" to being a "family."

Love is not finite. In the economy of human heart, you don't have to take love away from one person in order to share it with another. However, human energy and attention are very limited. We only have so much time and effort to commit before we need to rest. The reality is that in the first season of their lives, our children demand exorbitant amounts of consideration. These little people are entirely helpless and dependent on us as parents for care and comfort. And unless a mother suffers from some degree of postpartum depression or other illness or injury, she will most often choose her baby over her husband (and even herself) in this early season.

Now that can leave you (the new dad) feeling abandoned and neglected. You may even ask yourself the question, "Does my wife love the baby more than me?" Sometimes, maybe often, the answer to this question feels like, "Yes." And while in reality, she may not love the baby more than you, she probably feels immense gratitude, awe, and responsibility toward this new creature she brought into life through her body. For possibly the first time in her life, she has brushed up against the fullness of who she is as a woman and as an image bearer of God. She is different. You are different. Your marriage is different.

Being Chosen

I (David) remember swearing that we'd never ignore our dogs once we had children. I used to stand in judgment of those parents who had banished their canines to the backseat of the car or the backyard of the house. Heck, our chocolate lab once slept at the foot of our bed. Currently, she'd have to ask for directions to our bedroom if she ever got to come in the house. How did this happen?

Similarly, Connie and I vowed we wouldn't fall into the trap of a child-centered existence, and yet, we find ourselves fighting to find time with each other. It's a daily challenge to let the emphasis be on our relationship.

I can remember reading in books and discussing in childbirth classes how fathers begin to feel out of the loop during the early stages of a baby's development. My wife would reassure me, and I remember thinking, *Maybe those guys, but not me*. I was in for an awakening. I remember the first moment I felt outside of the sacred space my wife would share with each of our children. I felt as though I had nothing to contribute. Some moments I didn't even feel invited. Not only was I unwanted, I wasn't even missed. Everything my children needed could be provided for by my wife. I honestly felt a sense of not being missed. No one noticed me.

Being chosen and wanted is something so instinctive in us. Listen to the words of the Psalms:

> "For you created my inmost being;
> you knit me together in my mother's womb.
> I praise you because I am fearfully and wonderfully made; your works are wonderful,
> I know that full well. My frame was not hidden from you when I was made in the secret place.
> When I was woven together in the depths of the earth, your eyes saw my unformed body.
> All the days ordained for me
> were written in your book before one of the came to be.
> How precious to me are your thoughts, O God!

How vast is the sum of them!"
(Psalm 139:13-17).

Do you hear the psalmist's pleasure in being known and chosen in this passage? He speaks as a man who understands God's enjoyment for him and purpose in him. We long for this. I want my wife to want me (and not just in a physical manner). I want her to desire to be with me and to choose me. And yes, I want to be chosen over my children. I suspect you do as well. And she wants me to long for her in a similar way.

A Different Man for a Different Marriage

How are we to respond as men, husbands, and now fathers to this seismic shift in the tectonic plates of marriage? No matter how you look at your marriage, it's no longer "she and me." Whatever we are to do, we must move toward both our wives and children if we hope to create a relational structure that promotes a family alive to the wildness of life. As new dads, we respond to this change in a variety of ways. Sometimes our responses are helpful, and sometimes they are harmful. With so much newness, how are we to engage this new world order? If you think being a dad won't change your life, you are naive. If you entrench yourself in resistance to the changes that fatherhood brings, you are a stubborn mule.

Parenthood unalterably changes you. At its best, it softens our hearts, exposes our egos, and makes us more willing to sacrifice on behalf of the other in the cause of love. At its worst, we retreat into self-gratification, isolation, and independence. There are three common, harmful reactions that are hard to avoid, unless we are intentional in our responses.

COMPETITION

One harmful reaction to our new family role as dad is competition. Let us warn you plainly: This is not a contest! If you pit yourself against your child for the affection of your wife, you are setting up a relational dynamic that will harm your marriage and stifle your role as parent.

I (David) remember coming home one evening after work. I was spent. I drove home in this semiconscious state, wanting little to nothing expected of me. My body communicated an arrogant posture of, "I've spent the entire day sitting with people in pain . . . grief, loss, divorce, death, abuse, addiction, etc. . . . and I DESERVE to have little required of me."

If I dug a little deeper, underneath that statement was something like, "It's my turn now." This was tucked away somewhere as I ascended the stairs to my front porch. From my front door, there are two visible entry points. One is from a long hallway that pours into the front room of our house. The second opening is slightly to the right and comes from our kitchen into this front room. That evening, I could see both openings through the glass in the front door.

I found my little daughter running down the hall with her arms in the air yelling, "My daddy is home!" At just the same moment, my wife came out from the kitchen looking bedraggled and exhausted. Both would cross their respective openings at the same time. Behind my wife, I could see a kitchen full of dirty dishes, the table and floor full of the kids' leftover dinner. My wife's face said, "Get your butt in this house and give me some relief." My daughter's face seemed to say, "Pick me up and twirl me around because I want to be held by you!" Which opening do you think I wanted to move toward as I turned the key in the lock? I remember peering through the glass and thinking to myself, *I need to move toward my wife, although nothing in me wants to choose her right now.* First of all, my daughter beat her to the doorknob before I could push it open. I did twirl her around and enjoyed her delight in me. But that particular night, I was present enough to set her down after the greeting and to hold my wife in all her exhaustion.

Who do you love the most? The one who screams your name with delight or the one who wants to hand you over to dirty dishes and laundry? You are as capable as your wife of moving toward your children with all passion, intention, and creativity. It takes tapping into a source much larger than you are on a daily basis to move in a different direction. There is an incredible pull in us as parents toward our children—particularly in the early seasons of their development. They love boldly, they forgive easily, and they long for us passionately. They find comfort and security in our being. We find purpose and fulfillment in our place with them. These are things we lose and forget with our spouses.

But I must confess that many nights, I want to bypass her and the mess. Whether your wife does or does not choose you, your child needs to experience you choosing their mother over them. By choosing your wife first, you create an environment of safety and stability for your child.

SUBTERFUGE

Another way that some men cope with the full focus of their wife's attention being shifted is to knowingly or to unknowingly sabotage her relationship with their child. This often plays itself out in subtle ways, like in the case of one family we know. This father, unwilling to have his children be angry or hurt, refuses to take part in disciplining his children. He is willing to make his wife be the bad guy so that his children will see him as a good dad. However, this has inevitably driven a wedge between him and his wife. He has succeeded in disrupting his wife's relationship with his children. However, in the process, she has grown bitter, resentful, and tired. You cannot circumvent the bond of mother and child and bring any good into your life. To undermine your wife's relationship with your offspring is a violent reaction, and, if gone unchecked, will have long lasting impact on your family's future.

WITHDRAWAL

A third way we cope with the loss of our wife's attention is to withdraw: playing another round of golf, or staying later at work, or staring at the computer or TV. It is far too easy for us as men to skulk into the shadows when we perceive rejection. To cope, some of us turn to compulsions or addictions like work, exercise, masturbation, activities, television, pornography, reading, or whatever else that entertains and distracts our hearts.

It has taken me (Stephen) years to learn that my children and wife are more interested in my presence than my production. They want my passion and play over my profit and prestige. When feeling left out, I have more often than I'd like to admit retreated with filling my Palm Pilot and talking business on my cell phone in order to feel validated.

LOVING WELL

There is a better way. In order to succeed as both a husband and a father, you may need to search for a new entry into your wife's heart. Often in this new season, the most accessible way to her heart is through the category of family instead of couplehood. By stepping fully into fatherhood, she will more likely be drawn to you and unified with you.

To unleash the emotional and spiritual energy of our hearts on behalf of our wives and children requires love. And while love can be expressed in a number of ways, it always has four essential qualities. Love:

- delights in the presence of the other,
- has curiosity about the heart of the other,
- stands in the way of the other, and
- is willing to be hurt, but not harmed, by the other.

Delight is intended to mean celebrating the presence of the other and acknowledging their impact on relationship and reality. An example sounds like, "You are a great mom. I love how you _____ with our child."

Curiosity involves seeking to see and experience how your spouse is changing and being changed in the process. You might say, "What is this like for you, honey? What about being a mom scares you? What excites you?"

Standing in the way of is about setting boundaries with our spouses, as well as telling them the truth of our hearts. This would be like, "Honey, I know that leaving the baby with your mother makes you feel nervous, but I really need to have some time alone with you."

Love is also *sacrificial*. This may sound like, "Honey, I told Bob to go to the game without me. I really want you to go out and have some time that you need. Junior and I will be fine. Call Sally and go to dinner, a movie, and coffee afterwards."

Loving your wife and child well in this first season of family life will include exercising all four of these areas. What being a parent reveals, if you listen to your heart, is your continual need for personal transformation— becoming more of the man you long to become. But until we shift our focus from not sinning to loving well, we will fall short of our desire for our lives (specifically as husbands and fathers, but generally as men as well).

This all sounds so simple—loving well. So why aren't we able to move beyond ourselves and be the husbands and fathers we long to be? Our entire struggle begins with one question: Is God really good? The ultimate issue in marriage and parenting is not a failure to obey God, but rather a refusal to believe in, account for, and receive His generosity. In refusing to believe that God is good, we will disobey.

A token example is tithing (committing a tenth of everything earned to the local church). While this is a clear command in Scripture and tradition holds it as a central discipline in the Christian faith, statistics reveal that most Christians don't tithe. So what keeps us from it? For me (Stephen), my resistance to it is often fear. I don't believe that after I surrender 20-30 percent of my income to the government, put 15 percent toward retirement, and spend 25-30 percent on my mortgage that I will have enough money to make it through the month. I say to myself, "God is so big, He doesn't need this 10 percent as much as I will miss it." The issue at hand is not my disobedience; it's my fear. Truly, my 10 percent is ridiculously small when compared to the riches the Creator of the universe possesses. God doesn't need my money. God wants my heart.

What is at play here though is my unwillingness to grapple with the fact that I don't trust God's goodness—especially when it comes to money. On some level, I don't believe that He is generous enough or real enough to take care of me. And every time I doubt God's goodness, I sin, because it leads me off into my own planning and preparation apart from listening to Him. I will live safely, never risking the things that will free my heart.

Let's take another look at obedience through the lens of Genesis—specifically focusing on the curse. "To Adam he said, 'Because you listened to your wife and ate from the tree about which I commanded you, "You must not eat of it . . ."'"

Did you get that? His indictment of Adam was because he *listened* to her. God doesn't say, "Because you picked it . . . because you saw how good and beautiful and tasty it was . . . because it will increase your knowledge . . ." It doesn't say that. It says, "Because you listened to her." Is that an attack on the woman? No way. God is underscoring Adam's refusal to hear and then speak what he knew was right. It's like God is saying, "Not only did you listen to the wrong person, but you chose to be quiet." In Gen. 3 (the curse), God is coming after the one who's most at fault: Adam.

The term *curse* is so often misapplied here. Looking carefully at the text, we see that the only things cursed are the earth and the serpent. But apparently, they are not the ones responsible. The earth nurtured the tree; that's what the soil does. The serpent was slithery; that's who a serpent is. (Adam for sure knew the serpent's character, because Adam himself named him.)

The reverberations of Adam's inaction affected him, but also reshaped his world. Notice, too, that the description of Adam's consequences is twice as long as Eve's. God is very specific and intentional here. It's like He says, "Hey, let me say this one way. Then, let me say it again. And in case you don't quite get it, let me say it a third time." Here's what God says:

> Because you listened to your wife
> and ate from the tree
> That I commanded you not to eat from,

"Don't eat from this tree,"
The very ground is cursed because of you;
getting food from the ground
Will be as painful as having babies is for your wife;
you'll be working in pain all your life long.
The ground will spout thorns and weeds,
you'll get your food the hard way,
Planting and tilling and harvesting,
sweating in the fields from dawn to dusk,
Until you return to that ground yourself,
dead, and buried;
you started out as dirt, you'll end up as dirt.
(Gen. 3:17–19, MSG)

The flood of the curse unquestionably comes *to* man and woman and *through* man and woman. They reap the consequences of their disobedience: pain and suffering, toil and futility. But still, God's goodness prevails. It is very important to realize that Eve and Adam are not cursed specifically. In fact, God kills His own creation in order to give them clothing and protection for their lives outside the Garden. In this way, the curse and its consequences are redemptive. They are wrapped in the goodness of God.

FLEEING THE CURSE

If God is good, so are His actions, which means, to the degree you attempt to flee the curse, you flee from God. The attempt to flee the curse is to flee reality. So how do the consequences of our sin as men play themselves out in our lives? Another way to ask that same question is, "How do we flee the curse and distrust God's goodness?"

The first portion of the curse means that a man will experience a sense of futility. Everything a man does is to be hard. There alone is the explanation of the PowerBall and Lotto. Why do men fantasize about the lottery? Because it's easy. "For just one lousy dollar, I could get $100 million. I'd never have to work again." The second portion is, there will always be sweat and blood. The curse for a man will be that the earth breaks his back. The earth will always win. Men fantasize about the lottery because we want freedom from a world that breaks our backs. The world is rigged to break us and wear us down—and get this—God is the one who rigged it.

But more than work, there is another place that is more exhausting for us men. As relational beings, our primary sense of futility occurs with our wives and children. Paradoxically, they can also be our greatest source of joy.

God is far less concerned with *what* you do as a husband and father than He is with *how* you do it. What is the motivation of your heart? How and where do you doubt God's goodness? Where do you lack strength in your marriage? Where do you lack tenderness?

BE A HERO

While you may feel left out and unloved in the early days of parenting, there is a great relational opportunity for you as a father: being your child's hero. Everybody needs a hero—especially kids. They need someone to admire, follow, and hope in. While your wife will probably be your child's first choice when he is hurt or sick, you have the unique position as his hero.

Last night, my (Stephen) wife told me that she was talking with our daughter earlier in the day. They were working on finding a solution for some small problem when Emma Claire shouted out, "Mommy, let's call and ask daddy. He knows everything." While this may not have been what

Heather wanted to hear, she was wise enough to let my daughter believe in me.

Children want their father to be fun, strong, tender, and kind. For example, the other day, I was working from home and had just finished a conference call. It was later in the evening, and Heather was giving the kids a bath. I could hear laughter coming from the bathroom as I finished the call. Hanging up, I went into the bathroom to find Heather trying to convince them to begin washing. Upon my entrance, my children greeted me with celebration, cheers, and a lot of splashing. My response was to climb into the bathtub with all my clothes on. My son and daughter squealed with delight. It was a heroic response to a mundane situation.

There is a difference between heroes and idols. Heroes fight for justice and are compassionate. Heroes take risks and are brave. Heroes walk in humility and are modest. Idols are false gods and are powerless. Idols are propped up and phony. Idols are made in the image of man, not the image of God. Being your child's hero isn't about shoes you have to fill, because you are already in them. Your choice is to either stand up in those emotional and spiritual shoes or take them off.

Nursing and Feeding

When it comes to feeding a baby, there are two options: bottle or breast. For us men, nursing is bizarre. Breasts are supposed to be fascinating and fun—not functional! Your wife's breasts have enlarged throughout pregnancy, but you ain't seen nothing yet. Once your wife's milk comes in, you may literally be frightened by the size of them.

It takes a while to get the production regulated, and until then, your wife may be in great pain. Engorgement occurs when your wife's mammary glands first begin producing milk. This is when (in order to ensure that your baby doesn't starve) the "mams" go gangbusters.

Her breasts will be as hard as a sidewalk, and the only relief she can find—feeding the baby—will hurt so badly that it will bring tears to her eyes. This period of engorgement lasts only a few days, but it can feel like forever.

What can you do?

• See a lactation consultant at the hospital to learn proper nursing techniques. Watch closely, also, so that you can help your wife solve any problems that arise once you're home.

• Be gentle with your wife and ask her at each feeding what you can do to help. Be willing to jump in and do whatever she asks of you, even if it seems ridiculous. (You might have to draw the line at actually nursing the baby yourself.)

• Realize that it takes a while to get the hang of nursing. At the start, many babies take an entire hour to eat, which means that your wife sleeps only for two hours at a time. This will soon improve.

• Encourage your wife. By the time your baby is two months old, nursing will have become more routine and will not be such a production. Until that happens, your support, appreciation, kind words, and love will go a long way.

GRANDPARENTS AND FAMILY

There's no doubt about it: It is such a privilege to be able to introduce your parents (and other family members) to your new baby. No one else will celebrate their arrival with the same intensity and joy or be so willing to jump right in. However, the uncharted waters of grandparents can be more easily navigated with a bit of planning.

• Your relationship with your parents will change now that you're a parent. You may find that you disappoint your parents as you have to choose to do what is best for your own family rather than what would please others. Becoming a parent may also cause you to examine your relationship with your own parents and may bring up events and issues from the past that you need to deal with.

• It is important for you and your wife to outline your expectations clearly before the baby comes. Will you have family at the birth? Will someone stay with you when you come home from the hospital, or would you prefer to have some time alone with your spouse and the new baby? What will the grandparents' primary jobs be—holding the baby, feeding, cleaning, cooking? Decide upon these things as a couple and stick to them unless you both change your minds.

• If there is conflict with your extended family (including in-laws), you need to be the tough guy. Figure out how you can nicely set and enforce rules about baby care.

• Realize that no one is perfect. Your family will disappoint you just as you disappoint them. However, your children will delight in their grandparents, and you will laugh at how silly your parents can be when interacting with their beloved grandchildren. Remember that love covers a multitude of sins and enjoy this newest journey of being a son who is also a parent.

"I'm gonna be like you, Dad.
You know I'm gonna be like you."

—Harry Chapin,
"Cat's in the Cradle"

L arry had been married for about three years when he called me (Stephen) to inquire about counseling. When I asked him what spawned his call, he shared that his wife was having a baby in a few months, and he had some things he needed to figure out. We set up a time for the following afternoon and ended our call.

The next day, Larry was right on time, and as he walked through the door, he was in earnest conversation on his cell phone—a business call. "Yes, sir. I will check with the distributor and get back with you in about an hour. I'm sure we can work this out. Don't worry. It will be okay." He apologetically held his finger in the air as to say to me, "I'm sorry. It'll be just a second." I nodded, smiled, and waited patiently for him to finish up. I guessed Larry was in his late twenties, maybe early thirties, and was some kind of sales rep. He looked youthful and athletic. He donned a stubby goatee and was dressed in a striped golf shirt and khakis. When he finished his call, I greeted him and led him back to my office.

The first few moments of any new counseling relationship are awkward. You have complete strangers sitting across from each other. The client has chosen to come in usually because of some kind of emotional pain or relational problem. He is looking for help, and he has the expectation that this trained professional across from him is going to be able to provide it. Nowhere else does a relationship start with this as the landscape. As a counselor, I have grown

....

accustomed to the awkwardness of these first few minutes. I know that with a little curiosity on my part, even amid the strangeness of the moment, the client will usually pretty quickly move into a story of why he has come. That is why Larry's first words were so memorable.

"How are you? Are you doing okay today?" he asked me with genuine kindness.

I was off balance. *Hey! That's my question*, I thought to myself. "I'm doing well. Thank you for asking. It's been a great day so far." I replied. "How are you?"

"That's good to hear. I'm doing fine. I have this customer who is a little upset, but besides that, everything is going okay," He said with a bright smile.

"So tell me what brings you here today," I said. Larry replied with the customary self-descriptions used when making a new acquaintance. "I'm so-and-so old. My wife is named such-and-such. We've been married for however long. I do this kind of work." The depth of gentleness and consideration in his eyes struck me as he spoke of his wife and his faith and his work and how he came to call me. (His pastor referred him.) I remember thinking, *This is a really nice guy.*

"You mentioned on the phone that your wife is having a baby," I interrupted.

"Yes, a little girl. We are due in about twelve weeks. We are both really excited. We are going to name her Gracie." He paused and looked at me with a look that said, "What else would you like to know?" He was eager to comply with my questions.

"You said that you had some questions about that. How can I help?"

"We are just so thrilled," Larry said with a grin spread wide across his face. He paused again.

I decided to let the silence swell to see if he had more to say. He didn't.

"Larry," I began, "I know from experience that becoming a father can stir a lot of things in a man's heart: questions of competence, questions of ability, questions of mastery. What does your wife's pregnancy uncover in yours?"

He bit—hard. "My father left when I was six. He wasn't around much—if at all—when I was growing up. My mom remarried when I was twelve, to a guy named Mark. Mark was all right, but he could be mean, too. I realized last week that I don't know how to be a dad. No one taught me. What if I screw up another person's life?" Larry's smile melted, and tears pooled in his eyes.

My Heart is Wounded

Parenting affords us a chance to redeem our own childhoods by remembering our forgotten stories. Larry is not alone. If we are really honest, we have to admit that most of us come from a childhood where heartache was present. Our life stories contain themes of abuse and abandonment, moments of shame and sadness, and tales of death and despair.

There is something so unique about the opportunity we are given in parenting to reconnect with our own experience of being children. For many, this reconnection involves sadness, hurt, and disappointment. For some, reconnecting involves remembering trauma or abuse. For others, going back is a more nostalgic experience of reliving laughter and enjoyment.

As we live out our stories, we live out the stories of our parents. There is a direct link between our understanding of our own story and our experience in parenting. The more you understand of your own story, the more aware you are of what drives your response to your own children. Scripture implores us to acknowledge how we have been hurt and disappointed.

Psalm 109:21-22 states, "Deal well with me for your name's sake; out of the goodness of your love, deliver me. For I am poor and needy, and my heart is wounded within me." Your heart is wounded. This wounding was predicted. Life's pain is more fully addressed in Romans:

> The creation waits in eager expectation for the sons of God to be revealed. For the creation was subjected to frustration, not by its own choice, but by the will of the one who subjected it, in hope that the creation itself will be liberated from its bondage to decay and brought into the glorious freedom of the children of God.

> We know that the whole creation has been groaning as in the pains of childbirth right up to the present time. Not only so, but we ourselves, who have the first fruits of the Spirit, groan inwardly as we wait eagerly for our adoption as the sons, the redemption of our bodies. (Rom. 8: 19-24)

This is our guarantee: suffering and groaning. For those of you who have witnessed the pains of childbirth, you know how intense it is. For those of you who are expectant fathers, you will soon know the intensity of this pain. This pain is used as an analogy of the suffering we will experience this side of heaven. It is going to be bloody and messy, painful and hard. And we cannot escape it. We cannot separate ourselves from it. The ugly truth is that our children will experience this same painful wounding, and it will be at our hands.

What does groaning look like for you? You want to be connected with how being wounded gives way to groaning. You want to understand this because it impacts the man you are, the way you love your wife, and how you respond to your children.

As counselors, we see groaning in many different forms in our work with men and boys. When a man or a boy isn't connected with how he has been wounded, he is vulnerable to everything from substance abuse to sexual addiction. For Alex, being wounded involved his father ignoring his gifts artistically and ridiculing him publicly. His groaning comes in the form of interacting with women in chat rooms and nightly rituals of masturbating with magazines. For Mark, it looked like being emotionally entangled with his mother throughout his boyhood and adolescence. His desire to break away from her was violent and opened the door to using marijuana to help get through the day. For Jeff, having been wounded by his parents' divorce at eleven, he merely exists with his wife and kids. He provides well financially and is consistent in his role at home, but his wife cries out that she lives with a man who has checked out emotionally.

Outside of our experiences of counselors, here is what the raw data reveals:

- Half of all families are torn by divorce.
- Approximately one out of five adults struggle with some kind of addiction.
- Somewhere between 40 and 60 percent of all adults were victims of childhood/adolescent sexual abuse.
- Violence against women in the home causes more injuries to women than car accidents, muggings, and rape combined.

The odds are that you are somewhere in this mix. We all carry secret wounds from the family we grew up in, secrets that shape who we become as men and therefore as fathers. We all have different ways of resigning from our hearts. Even if you somehow escaped the tragedy of a broken home or the betrayal of abuse, it is impossible to escape the sin of your parents. They were not perfect. And guess what: You can't be either.

We desperately hope that your sin against your child does not severely damage his/her heart. But we know that you will wound him/her. You have the opportunity, through understanding your family of origin, to not repeat some of the same relational harms that were perpetrated on you. But without stepping into your story (and inviting God and others to join you there), you will most certainly repeat the sins of your parents with your own child.

Two questions you must wrestle with if you hope to parent well are: (1) Where do I come from? and (2) What's my marriage like?

What Was Your Childhood Like?

As you consider your own childhood and reflect on who your parents were, what stories fill your heart? What are the themes? What is similar in your most prominent childhood memories? What is distinct?

What kind of family you grew up in greatly influences your parenting style. To get a picture of how you want to father, consider first how your parents shaped and molded you. While I was in graduate school at Mars Hill, I heard author, speaker, and psychologist Dan Allender in lectures suggest asking these two questions: "Was I loved?" and, "Could I get my own way?" There are four possible combinations when answering these two questions. Each response describes a distinct parental style.

Yes, I was loved/
Yes, I could get my own way.

If this describes how your parents engaged you as a boy, then you felt prized. There are probably pictures of you in a gown as a baby. You were mom and dad's little prince. If this was your childhood, you were likely indulged and spoiled. You were bought things. You were sent off to camp. Your life was made easy and wonderful. You were a stranger to heartache.

Does it still feel like love? To a degree. Is it really love? Not in the least.

You learned to whine, to wrap your mother around your little finger, or you were your father's little man. You learned how to manipulate. Sometimes you were sweet. Sometimes you were demanding. But more often than not, you knew how to get what you needed. If this is you, you have had very caring parents—perhaps to the point of absorbing you. The world revolved around you. An atmosphere where a child is permitted to get his or her own way is seldom an environment grounded in wisdom and strength.

Children of these parents possess charisma, sophistication, and charm. These kids have the ability to be supportive and mature in adult-like settings and present a comfortable know-how. However, this confidence is just a ruse. Underlying this façade is a well of significant shame. This shame is deeply rooted in an experience of uncertainty, because all the goods of life have come without having to be strong, to be competent, or to suffer. If there was a problem in math or on the team, your parents went to talk to your teacher, who didn't give you a good grade, or your coach, who wouldn't let you play enough.

If this was your childhood, deep down, you felt stronger than your parents. As a child, you sensed at a very core level that your parents were/are afraid of you. This means you are the strongest person in the world, and you happen to know that you are not that strong. So if you're the strongest person in the world and you're not that strong, you have to put on a façade. You have to project a lot more competence than you indeed feel yourself to have. Therefore, you constantly feel like a fake. Your fear is that you're going to be found out. Your shame is hidden under charisma and charm.

No, I wasn't loved/
Yes, I could get my own way.

If your answer to these two questions was "No" and "Yes," then yours was a home in which your parents did not care what you did. This was a family without rules and boundaries, though there may have been the pretense of rules. "You must make As and Bs," but nobody ever checked your report card. One term, you brought home three Cs and a D, and no one said a word. The next term, you brought home an A, two Bs, and a D, and all hell broke loose. You never questioned, "Why?" You understood that insanity was the point. The rules changed every minute as did the consequences.

No one enjoyed you. No one treasured your presence. You felt/feel like an inconvenience. There was more than likely some kind of abuse: be it physical, emotional, verbal, or sexual. Chaos reigned. This was not a happy family. It was probably an addictive, impulsive, and violent home. In this family, more than likely there was a history of abuse, conflict, addiction, and heartache. There may have even been a history of mental illness.

No, I WASN'T LOVED/ No, I COULDN'T GET MY OWN WAY.

Are you loved? Not really. Can you get your way? Never. If this was/is you, you likely came from a well-to-do home with well-educated parents, probably with financial excess. It was the typical suburban, upper-middle class family. This was the good Christian, conservative, Republican home.

Are there rules in this house? Yes. Hard and fast rules. Do the kids obey these rules? You better believe it. If a rule is broken, there are consequences that are certain and final. Are you loved? How dare you ask that question? Love is dutiful in this family—it is required.

If this was your childhood, you spent your time being driven by a set of rules and tasks that had to be performed. You were/are constantly asking the question of others, "What do you want?" In school, you panicked when a teacher assigned a paper, and you probably asked twenty questions about how she wanted the paper done. At work, you are diligent and more than likely work for a tyrant (unless you are the tyrant). You were/are looking to perform. "Tell me the rules, and I will follow them." The result is a life marked by emptiness and stress.

As an adult, you don't know who you are, and you don't know what you want, unless you have constructed an elaborate web of rules and motivators. You lack any idea of what it means to choose to be free. You resist asking life's hard questions. Why? Because you were raised in an environment that was like a prison.

As an adolescent, you probably longed for the chance to escape, but you never could, because to do that meant you would shatter your family. Almost always in one of these homes, there is one child who will break out. This is the sister or brother who everybody loves to hate (but all of the siblings really envy). This is the child who the family prays for and hopes that God returns him or her to being normal like everyone else. As a child from this family, you don't ask questions, and you don't think about issues. Either mom or dad provided every answer. In many instances, this is a fundamentalist home run by fear and shame with the ultimate promise of, "We'll take care of you, as long as you obey us."

Yes, I was loved/ No, I couldn't get my way.

This is from where we as fathers hope to parent. The reality is that while we may wander into this area on occasion, it is hard to stay here. Our hope as fathers is to create a context where our children feel loved, but know that they can't escape the consequences of reality. This is a model of parenting that is marked by consistency and humility.

In a family that is driven by this parenting framework, mom and dad don't have all the answers, but they are willing to ask life's hard questions with their children. Most of us did not come from this type of home. Our hope is, however, to move our own families toward a style of living that is defined by tenderness and strength. Like your parents were with you, how you and your wife interact will define in large part how you will parent. If you are able to offer your child a home where he feels loved but cannot get his own way, you have moved a long way toward uncovering the image of God in his soul.

What Kind of Husband are You?

Who are you? What characteristics and attitudes describe your relational style? As a man, how do you tend to encounter the chaos of life? Are you a peacemaker or a boat rocker? Do you watch with curiosity, or do you dive right in? Would most people describe you as a gentleman or a roughrider? In exploring your own style of relating, there are two helpful categories to consider. Each of these categories is on opposite ends of the same continuum.

MR. NICE GUY   ▼   JOE QUARTERBACK

10   8   6   4   2   0   2   4   6   8   10

On one end is Mr. Nice Guy. He is often well-liked, but not much respected. This guy is defined by the idea of a man who avoids taking hold of life.

In the romantic comedy *Along Came Polly* starring Ben Stiller and Jennifer Aniston, Mr. Nice Guy would be Stiller's character, Reuben Feffer. In the movie, Reuben works as a senior risk analyst for an elite life insurance underwriter. The tool of Reuben's trade is the "Riskmaster," an insurance analysis software of his own design. It is programmed to compare risk and rewards of his clients to see if their lives contain too much risk to be insurable. Reuben is a man who blots the grease off his pizza, avoids walking on sidewalk grates, and won't eat the mixed nuts at a bar. Reuben knows that "when you think you're innocently eating a little bar snack, you're actually ingesting potentially deadly bacteria from about thirty-nine soiled strangers."

Mr. Nice Guy refuses to initiate things and resists risk. While usually safe and trustworthy, he is most often passionless and emotionally impotent. He has others enter life's fray on his behalf because he's shown he can't do it for himself.

On the other end of the spectrum is Joe Quarterback. Joe is usually respected (feared) and popular, but seldom ever liked. He is a man who is intentional, driven, and competent. He often possesses an elegance and flair to how he makes life work. Most often a "Type A," Joe Quarterback is driven by success and is perceived to be a good CEO or entrepreneur. He has been known to use violence or threats of violence (harsh words, finger pointing, door slamming) so that other people comply with his will.

We each are somewhere on this spectrum. We all tend toward one end or the other. Sometimes we are different on different days, and sometimes we are different with different people. In general, we can usually find ourselves leaning to either the right or left of the center. Where are you? Where is your father?

What Kind of Wife is She?

With some idea of your relational style, it is helpful to also understand how your wife engages life. Like men, women, too, exist on a continuum.

Anchoring one end is the Mrs. Good Girl. This is a woman busy making sure life is good for those around her. She is dispassionate and may even seem helpless. She likes to be taken care of, and she often has someone else do for her what she cannot do. Unlike the Mr. Nice Guy, Mrs. Good Girl may engage conflict, but she will allow someone else to make the decisions about the solution. On this spectrum, you might find Carol Brady from the seventies TV sitcom, *The Brady Bunch*.

Balancing Mrs. Good Girl is Ms. Busy Lady. Ms. Busy Lady is seen as competent, confident, and organized. She can both bring home the bacon and fry it up in the pan, and you better not have a blamed thing to say about it. She may humiliate or verbally assault others, and she has been known to make others pay (especially men) for being alive and having desire. Think Martha Stewart.

MRS. GOOD GIRL ▼ MS. BUSY LADY

WHEN A MAN MEETS A WOMAN?

These are only rough categories based on Allender's work. And while only rough outlines, they can still give us some perspective of our spouse and ourselves. By combining the four personality archetypes, we get four possibilities for marriage. It is likely you will find your wife and you somewhere in one of these categories.

MR. NICE GUY/MRS. GOOD GIRL

This is the couch marriage. Husband and wife come home from work. They make dinner, then they watch a *Seinfeld* rerun, *Who Wants to Be a Millionaire*, maybe the latest *CSI Miami*, and then the local news. Most always, they are in bed at the same time. This is the marriage that's tiresome, exhausting, and predictable. If you are a Nice Guy and you're married to a Good Girl, you can understand how boring your marriage is at times. Conflict? Oh sure, you fight, but everybody "makes up" in the end (and no one ever goes to bed angry). When children come along into this family, they often look for ways to create havoc or excitement. They fantasize about burning the house down to see if anyone notices.

Joe Quarterback/Mrs. Good Girl

This is a Promise Keepers marriage. There is a very kind woman married to a very strong man. She greets her husband in the morning with a hot cup of coffee, a warm smile, and a kiss on the cheek. He can be a little ferocious, but he can also be a lot of fun. He's in charge, and people respect him. He is usually on a committee or two at church and goes to Rotary on Thursday mornings. He's got a stack of pornography hidden in the bottom of his sock drawer or on the computer. Everybody knows it, but nobody says a word about it. Once kids enter the picture, this is a home where dad gets excused, and it's always mom's fault.

Mr. Nice Guy/Ms. Busy Lady

This is the typical twenty-first century, American family. This is a home that is upwardly mobile. You find a kind man and a wise, worldly woman who's bringing energy to the relationship. She always aspires to the next level. The husband regularly feels brow beaten or tongue lashed. The children of this couple may have a lot of sympathy and pity for dad and a sense of respect for mom. They would rather be with dad, but they also know if mom explodes, dad won't protect them. He feels sad for you, but you can't count on him. As long as the children don't rob a bank, they are going to be left alone, but they have to be successful.

Joe Quarterback/Ms. Busy Lady

This is an interesting couple. This is a very distant marriage, but they have a great time together. They don't see one another regularly—even when in the same room. They enter into their Palm Pilots when their week at the coast will be. They eat out. They enjoy power lunches. They're both successful, and they're making things work. They both enjoy an active sex life. It is just usually with someone besides his or her spouse. These couples don't have kids. (If they do, it is usually only one, and they send her off to boarding school when she is six.)

Stepping onto the Court

I (David) grew up in a small southern town, Shelbyville, Tennessee. It is the Walking Horse Capital of the world, as well as the Pencil Capital of the World. And it's infamous for high school girls basketball. (We have been national champions on several occasions.) It is a rural community with Deep South values and smalltown charm. When I was growing up, it was safe to ride your bike in the street, everyone knew your family, and you could travel from one end of town to the other in ten minutes or less. The rhythm of life was slow.

In the spring of 1979, I began my basketball career. My first step was playing point guard for Burger Chef, one of the local burger joints in town. (A local establishment sponsored each team.) We played Saturday games at the old elementary school gymnasium. It was a nine-man team with two coaches. I was the smallest boy on the team, and it would be safe to say the weakest asset. Every Saturday, my parents would load our family into the car and drive over to watch me sit on the bench for three quarters, only to be put in for ten minutes of the fourth so that I could maintain my status as a team member. My favorite part of the experience was the chocolate shake and skinny fries at Burger Chef following the game. Needless to say, I didn't go on to play college ball or enter the NBA.

Despite not having any genetic gifting, my boys seem to love the game of basketball. At eighteen months, we would walk down the hall of the YMCA, and they would peer through the glass at the court, point, and shout "basketball!" (Which sounded something like "ssskatball.") We began a ritual around that time where I would drop them off at the Y childcare, I would squeeze in a workout, and then we would all three file into the gym to shoot some hoops. They would scream every time I stripped the net, chase after the ball, and bring it back for me to do it again. They loved to watch the pickup games taking place in the court next to us. This ritual is still a part of our morning routine a couple of days a week.

One Monday morning, I was holding one of the boys on my shoulders as he attempted to throw the ball. It occurred to me that at some point in the not-so-faraway future, my boys will discover that their dad ended his basketball career (and skill, for that matter) as a ten-year-old point guard for Burger Chef. The Magic Johnson they experienced me to be at eighteen months of age isn't so magical on the court. I realized, standing mid-court with a boy on my shoulders holding a basketball, that the realities of my incompetence will be exposed in a matter of years.

For so long, I was a man disconnected from my story and my heart. I was a man who wouldn't ask questions. This opened the door to many destructive possibilities. One of the very reasons we wanted to write a book that involved asking questions was that we believe this kind of pursuit leads to connection. Asking these questions will involve exploring your story and connecting with your heart. Otherwise, you will be vulnerable and reckless.

Unless I go back and reconnect with the pain of being the smallest guy benched in most every basketball game played, nothing in me will want to step onto the court with my sons. I will live in fear of the idea of a pickup game with those boys. Something in me will instinctively move away from that experience of connecting with them and other similar experiences.

Fear is enormous in us as men. We are afraid of the power we don't have. We are often afraid of the power we *do* have. Fear is paralyzing. The fear of power or lack of power is what keeps many men from entering into the marriage relationship. This same fear keeps many men from desiring to have children. And it is this fear that keeps men disengaged from the experience of parenting.

We believe stepping onto the court is a call to remember. Remember your experiences of playing. Remember your experiences of failing. Remember your experiences of succeeding. Remember who yelled to you from the sidelines. What kinds of words did you hear? My friend Jerry well remembers playing high school ball. His dad's presence at his games was more of a curse than a blessing. His dad would show up intoxicated. He would scream at him from the sidelines. It humiliated Jerry in front of his peers.

What if no one was yelling? No one showed up at the game to cheer you on. What if, like me, you didn't get into the game often enough to hear the chanting from the stands? You heard the noise, but no one was yelling your name. Regardless of what you did or didn't hear, regardless of who was absent or present, it is important to remember. As men, we are called by God to remember. He speaks to remembering in Deuteronomy:

> "Only be careful, and watch yourselves closely so that you do not forget the things your eyes have seen or let them slip from your heart as long as you live. Teach them to your children and to their children after them." (Deut. 3:9)

Frederick Buechner powerfully writes of this in his memoir, *Telling Secrets*,

> ". . . memory makes it possible for us both to bless the past, even those parts of it that we have always felt cursed by, and also to be blessed by it. If this kind of remembering sounds like what psychotherapy is about, it is because it is, but I think it is also what the forgiveness of sins is all about—the interplay of God's forgiveness of us and our forgiveness of God and each other."

It is through memory that we are able to reclaim much of our lives that we have long since forgotten or buried. Telling my (David) story reminds me of the power of redemption. I am reminded of a God who breaks through the groaning and the wounding. Not only does He break into it, but He also transforms it into something valuable and purposeful. Note that there is no disclaimer in that passage of Deuteronomy. There is nothing that says, "You can forget the things your eyes have seen if they have been harmful." There is no separate category for "letting things slip from your heart if they wounded you." We are called to remember our entire story.

> *Piece together these little mysteries*
> *It isn't hard to see the writing on the wall*
> *Triumph and tragedy, only God can be*
> *Both the builder and the wrecking ball*
> —"Wrecking Ball" by Andy Bullhorn

Collect your story. Name the truth of your past: both the beautiful and the ugly. Share it with your wife. Grab a ball. Step onto the court. Get in the game. Get used to the idea that you will wound your child's heart and bruise his soul. That is no reason to sit on the bench.

Finances

• Communication is critical! Set apart a time each month to review the current month's spending, and plan your spending for the upcoming month. If your relationship is like most, one of you is a saver and the other is a spender. Be forewarned—the spender may cry at these monthly meetings. If you are the saver, be gentle with your spender. Remind her that it is okay to spend—you just have to plan it first.

• Think long-term. There is a lot of baby stuff for sale, but not all of it is necessary. You can reduce later stress and anxiety by making wise spending decisions now.

• Make a preliminary budget for after baby by estimating the new expenses you will have. You can probably count on at least $100-$200 per month for ongoing expenses.

• When money is tight, many couples tend to start cutting back on unnecessary spending. That is a great idea, unless it means that you no longer have time together to build your relationship. You don't have to spend much, but make it a priority to date and appreciate each other.

What major things do you need to have in place?

1.) A will—You can do a quick one with a computer program.

2.) Life insurance—for both you and your wife

3.) Disability insurance—may not be necessary if you have enough savings to be self-insured

4.) Emergency savings—about six months of your monthly expenses saved to meet unexpected expenses

5.) Education fund for baby

Money saving tips:

1.) Buy at consignment sales: gently used=much less expensive.

2.) Buy diapers, wipes, and formula at wholesale clubs.

3.) Shop for baby clothes, gifts, etc., when they are on sale; buy bigger sizes for next year's wardrobe for baby.

Essentials for Baby and Product Guide

Things to Remember When Purchasing

• Buy larger sizes, too. Newborn clothes may not fit for long; of course, that is dependent on your child's size at birth and how quickly he or she grows.

• Remember that even if you have a fairly big baby, it will still seem that most clothes are too big. Rest assured, they will fit soon!

• Make sure the crotch opens easily for diaper changes—especially on pajamas. You'll be changing lots of diapers in the middle of the night.

Miscellaneous

- **3 hooded towels**
- **6 washcloths**
- **2 crib sheets**
- **waterproof mattress pads**
- **bassinet sheets if needed**
- **baby soap and shampoo**
- **brush and comb**
- **baby nail clippers**
- **thermometer**
- **rubbing alcohol for umbilical cord**
- **petroleum jelly for circumcision**
- **diaper rash ointment**
- **diapers**—Don't buy too many in newborn size—once their diaper begins leaking, it's time to move up to the next size. This will happen quickly.
- **wipes**
- **baby bathtub**
- **humidifier**—optional, depending on how dry your air is
- **monitor**
- **mobile**—Be sure to look at it from below—your baby's perspective—as you choose it.
- **music for the nursery**
- **lamp or nightlight**—for late-night diaper changes
- **bouncy seat**

swing—a great thing to borrow, since it's impossible for you to know if your child will like it

Pack 'N Play

1 dozen cloth diapers—to be used as burp cloths

Myliconä drops—for when your baby is screaming, and you just want to be able to do something!

FURNITURE

crib—Make sure it meets all safety standards if it is used.

bassinet—not necessary, but fun if you want to have one; will not last long!!

changing table, dresser, etc.—place to change diapers and store clothes

rocker/glider/chair—for feeding, reading, snuggling, etc.

www.babybargains.com—You may want to get the latest version of *Baby Bargains* by Denise and Alan Fields. It's a great resource for finding cheaper ways to get all the gear. Plus, it rates all baby products currently available on the market.

"Parenthood is a lot easier to get into than out of."

—Bruce Lansky

CHAPTER 7
WHAT IF MY HOUSE IS TOO SMALL?

Babies bring change, not the least of which is financial. Babies are big business. Each year in the U.S., more than $1 billion is spent on diapers alone. And guess who pays for all that? New parents.

With the addition of children comes myriad new things: toys, clothes, diapers, carriers, furniture, and a variety of other devices and equipment (most of which we don't really need, but we buy anyway). But it doesn't stop there. Those are the initial purchases. What is less obvious but more of a financial hit are the other expenses: life insurance, college funds, childcare, added health insurance, and grocery bills. This is where the real cost is. To raise a child today in America (birth to seventeen years) costs approximately $180,000.

As fathers, much of how we identify ourselves is anchored in our ability to provide well for our families: seeing that our children live in the right houses, ride in the right cars, go to the right schools, and wear the right clothes. While some of this thinking is tied to Western materialism, it is more rooted in our desire as fathers to provide our children with the things that make them safe, secure, comfortable, and happy. No father in his right mind would say, "I want my son to live in poverty, use drugs, be uneducated, and feel depressed." At the core, we are stamped in the image of God, and like Him, we want only the best for our children. The problem comes when this desire for our children's best is in conflict with our own well-being. Somehow, being a parent will always reveal these moments of discord.

There is a hilarious moment in the movie *Nine Months* that captures this sentiment. In a scene entitled "Life-Changing Events," Sam and Rebecca are leaving the hospital following their first OBGYN appointment. They have inconveniently run into an overbearing couple, Marty and Gail (Tom Arnold and Joan Cusack), who are also pregnant, but with their fourth child. The two couples are making their way across the street to their cars making small talk.

Gail: How are you feeling?

Rebecca: I'm okay. I've been a little tired.

Marty: Everybody gets tired.

Rebecca: Sure.

Marty: It's just that the whole thing is such a life-changing event.

Gail: I'll give you my number. Call me.

Rebecca: I'd like that.

Gail: We can go baby shopping and have lunch. And you've got to get that book . . . *What to Expect When You're Expecting*.

Marty: And we've got some great videos you can watch because we've filmed every one of our births. You've got to film your first one 'cause that's the best because it's the bloodiest, you know. Blood everywhere, things are shooting in and out. People are screaming. Stuff's getting torn apart and sewed together. It's like a really good World War II movie.

The four come to a stop in front of Sam's prized possession (and recently rebuilt) Porsche 911 cherry-red convertible. The scene cuts to Marty and Sam.

Marty:	So, you going to keep the car?
Sam:	Yeah, it's fine now. Cost a bit of money, but it's only three months old.
Marty:	But it only seats two people.
Sam:	It always did.
Marty:	Yeah right, but you are going to have a baby now. So you're gonna need something bigger.
Gail:	You could never fit a car seat in there. You don't have enough seat belts.
Marty:	I don't even know where the trunk is (pointing to the car). Listen. Stop down by the lot. I'll make you a good deal. All right?
Sam:	Great. *(He says dejectedly, his face thickly painted with nausea and disgust.)*

Marty and Gail turn and walk away.

Marty:	Come on, baby. Let's roll. See you guys.

Sam is left standing with Rebecca. His disgust has melted to rage.

Sam:	I hate him. I loathe him. I detest him. You know he just tried to sell me a new car. Can you believe that? Tacky or what?
Rebecca:	Yeah, you know, but he is right. We're gonna need something bigger— something with four seats.
Sam:	But Rebecca, you know how much I love my car. I've worked hard for it.
Rebecca:	*(Angry now.)* Well, what do you suggest we do? Tie the baby to the hood like a deer?

Sam:	(Looking bewildered.) Well, no, but maybe you could get your own car.
Rebecca:	On my salary? Come on.
Sam:	Well, put it this way. I'm not getting rid of the car. Simple as that.
Rebecca:	What about the cat?
Sam:	(Sam is now enraged.) Just wait! You said this baby wouldn't have to change our lives. Now suddenly, I have to sell my car and get rid of the cat I've had for sixteen years. This is the second month, and our lives are practically unrecognizable!

Fish or Cut Bait

Like Sam, no matter how much we all may want it to be different, life is not stagnate. Life is full of change. It is always changing, unfolding before us into something new. Often this new thing is familiar enough that it isn't overwhelming, and other times it is unrecognizable. Sam's resistance was more about fighting his lack of control over change. The same is true for the rest of us. We cannot stop change. We are always caught up in the process of becoming something different. In fact, we are made for change. God has designed us as evolving creatures equipped to move into the mystery of the unknown. Theologically, this is called sanctification. Practically, it's called parenthood.

At the core of every man are two competing desires: adventure and security. This reality explains roller coasters, action-adventure movies, and rock climbing with safety gear. We want to experience excitement and safety simultaneously. We feel most alive when things seem out of control. We feel most secure when outcomes are predictable and manageable.

One big way we try to control life and manage the experience of chaos is through money. Like Sam, much of our emotional and spiritual wrangling takes place in the realm of the material. I (Stephen) have told myself numerous times that once I was making X amount of money, life would be okay. Or once I had these bills paid, things would be better. Every time, I have been thwarted in my planning.

During the process of writing this book, my wife and I bought a house. It is a smallish three-bedroom, two-bath brick ranch on a quiet street in a great neighborhood. It is perfectly cozy for Heather and me, our two children, and our chocolate lab. It has a great backyard shaded by huge oak and walnut trees. There is this creek that runs beside the house where Heather dreams of planting flowers along the bank. Three months after we moved in, we learned we were pregnant with our third child. We had been talking about the possibility of a new baby for many months. When it did finally happen, it was incredibly exciting news. But with the change in our family, there also was some anxiety—okay, a lot of anxiety.

As I begin to consider this future addition, I have a growing fear that where we live is way too small. Heather assures me we can make it work (for the next few years anyway). The car issue is a totally different subject, however. Heather and I both drive automobiles that are more than ten years old. But besides the consumption of oil each month, both run pretty reliably. So, that is not really the problem. Our challenge is more one of volume, not condition.

As it stands now, neither of our cars will hold three car seats. When the new baby is born, our other two children will be five and two. Law requires that they remain in car seats or booster seats until they reach eighty-five pounds. That is three car seats in the backseat—impossible for our cars. I am left to buy a new car with money I don't have.

To top off my money fears, Heather's health insurance won't cover the birth. That means paying for the doctor and hospital out-of-pocket. No co-pay, no deductible this time around. We are left with a house that we have to either add onto or sell sometime in the next three years, having to buy a new car, and funding a delivery with cash. Yikes!

The way I see it, this new baby will cost me somewhere between $125,000 to $200,000 when all is said and done . . . a cost that is a bargain when I consider the joy of being a father, but talk about being out of control!

When 1 + 1 = 3

I (David) have a similar story. I remember well the day we had our first ultrasound with our second pregnancy . . . the day we found out there were two babies growing inside my wife when we had believed for months there was only one. I can remember where I was standing when I called my parents to tell them this news. I remember everything in our world changed in an instant.

One of the exciting parts of having a second child for us as dads is when we realize we already own (and have already assembled) most all of the paraphernalia—the gear, the baby bed, the stroller, the car seat, the Pack 'N Play, the high chair, the backpack or jogging stroller, the Diaper Genie, the changing table, the ExerSaucer, the umbrella stroller, the bassinet, and on and on and on. The investment of time and money has been made, and we're ready to get some more mileage out of all this junk that takes up every square foot of our house. One of the many devastating realities of finding out you're having multiples is that you get to buy one more of EVERYTHING! If you are having triplets or quads, increase the numbers as needed.

I was shattered by the idea of purchasing again. Not even the stroller works. Now we need a double stroller! Everything would increase proportionally, with the exception of my income. One of the many realities to come crashing in on us as we digested the news of two babies was the reality that just two years prior to this surprise, we had decided to downsize so that my wife could transition out of her full-time teaching career into a new career of being a stay-at-home mother and part-time tutor. We had made a decision to sell our two-story house and move into a little 1930s cottage in an urban, historical neighborhood that we loved. We bought a house with a thousand square feet, tons of charm, two bedrooms, one bath, and one closet. We didn't need much space, and we loved the idea of being together in close quarters with our new little family. We even dreamed of bringing home another infant somewhere down the road, and it still being enough space for a family of four, as long as the children were small. We'd graduate to something bigger down the road when we had more resources (like that day would ever come, but we were dreamers and surveying in the beauty of being pregnant for the first time).

It was a perfect plan if life worked the way I desperately needed it to, but it wasn't designed to work that way. So there we sat at the OBGYN appointment, trying to breathe and recover from the news of having multiples in four months. On the way home from the appointment, I called our realtor and friend, Amy Barnes. The call sounded a bit like a 9-1-1 call. "Amy, we're having twins, and we need to sell this house, buy a new one, and move in the next sixty to ninety days. Can you come over immediately?" Thankfully, Amy Barnes is graceful, calm, and thoughtful. She responded to our 9-1-1 call, and we managed to list our house, sell it, and buy a new one in thirty days. Did

I mention that she is a magician? I don't know how it happened, but we somehow accomplished all those things in a month. I do know how it happened. It was the grace of God and the help of amazing friends who came to our rescue. Did I mention that the house we bought needed renovating?

The house was the first of many discoveries that we didn't have enough space to make it work. At the time, I was driving a Nissan Sentra. My wife was driving the same Toyota Camry she had been driving since she started graduate school. And in case you are wondering, three car seats won't really fit in the backseat of either of those vehicles. Actually, if someone stands at each back door and you count to three and slam them shut at the same moment, it can be done. However, we weren't certain what the long-term neurological effects would be for our children if we were to continue that practice. So I started entertaining the need to buy a larger vehicle and how to also deliver pizzas on the weekends to pay for all the expense.

I did a long Internet search to accomplish some of the mandatory research involved in purchasing a new vehicle. I would literally show up at dealerships and ask the sales guys to help me see if three car seats would sit in the backseat with both doors able to shut easily. Can I just tell you that there are only a handful of vehicles that will meet that requirement? You see, by the time most people have a third child, their oldest is either out of a car seat or in some skinny little booster seat. Not my three little people. We are talking full-on, rear facing, big honkin' car seats. The kind that you could snowboard on or use as a flotation device for a family of six. Can you imagine the looks I got when I started hauling these seats out of my trunk and handed them over to some sales guy who is thinking to himself, *No amount of commission is worth this guy*? It was a long, arduous process, but I am now the proud owner of a used Ford Expedition, big enough to haul a family of five with plenty of room for all our paraphernalia. And we have a lot of gear.

The paraphernalia is a point of tension in our household. My wife and I have different opinions on baby gear. I come from the old school. My thinking is: "People survived for thousands of years without the ExerSaucer, and babies lived and grew to be productive members of society." My wife, on the other hand, believes that if Babies R Us stocks it, we have a need for it, and our children's development may be stunted without it.

SUFFICIENCY

For much of my (Stephen) marriage, whenever Heather and I argue, there is often a consistent theme. Over the course of our relationship, as we have grown together, this conflict has become more honest, more accurate, and more loving. Usually this conversation has to do with a combination of two topics: money and time.

Since we've had children, Heather has been a stay-at-home mom, and it has been my responsibility to generate income. While God has been more than faithful in sustaining us financially, there have been times when resources have been scarce—in other words: We've been broke. And as with many couples, in my marriage, money issues can create fear. In my marriage, I generally fend off my fear with anger and shame. When tensions rise around money, I almost always feel humiliated. I tell myself, "If I was a real man, I'd provide better for my family." To fend this off, I get angry with Heather, and it becomes far too easy for me to feel things like, "If you would just get a job . . ."

But money in and of itself is rarely the sole issue.

While Heather is very supportive of my career and my interests, she is even more passionate about our family—especially our children. As the sole bread winner and a workaholic, I often commit to being over-committed. Heather has facetiously labeled this as "Palm Pilot-itis." This is a debilitating aliment where the sufferer (me) is uncontrollably compelled to fill in any blanks in his calendar. This is compounded with the fact that I really love my work. It becomes easy for me to be gone from home. While my greatest passion is for my family, much of my identity and gratification comes from work.

When these two issues (money and time) come to bear in the same conversation, it is awful. It sounds something like this:

Heather will say, "I wish we had more storage space." Which I will hear as, "If you were a real man, we'd have a bigger house."

I'll say, "I know. Me, too. Is there anything we can give away?" By that I mean, "I'm working as hard as I can. What more do you want?"

She will respond, "You haven't spent any one-on-one time with the kids this week. I thought it would be a good chance for me to get away for a few hours and for you and the kids to connect." Which I hear as, "Where have you been? You suck as a father."

This is a vicious cycle that obviously hits some pretty sensitive places in my story. But I have talked to enough men to know that it is not all that unfamiliar.

I am convinced that this difference in opinion has some root in my sense of who I am. As strange as it may sound, I believe my perspective is rooted in the fear that I am insufficient. I can't handle it on my own. I don't have what it takes. The house is too small.

If I am a real man, I will provide for my family, my wife won't ever need to work again, my children can attend the college of their choice, and my dog can be groomed at an upscale pooch parlor. The reality is that I can't provide those things for my family. Nor would having that ability be the solution. Yet still I live as if I believe it is the solution. If only I made more, we'd be set. If only I could replace my beat-up Accord with something new, we'd be taken care of. My list goes on and on and on.

Eventually my thinking turns into, "God, why don't You show up? How are we going to pay for unexpected repairs? How are these kids going to go to college? How will I fund our retirement?" Scripture tells the account of Habakkuk, a minor prophet who asked God a similar question and then waited for a response.

> What's God going to say to my questions? I'm braced for the worst. I'll climb to the lookout tower and scan the horizon. I'll wait to see what God says, how he'll answer my complaint.
>
> And then God answered: "Write this. Write what you see. Write it out in big block letters so that it can be read on the run. This vision-message is a witness pointing to what's coming. It aches for the coming—it can hardly wait! And it doesn't lie. If it seems slow in coming, wait. It's on its way. It will come right on time." (Hab. 2:1-3, MSG)

WAIT! Wait? Wait on it because it's on its way. I despise that message. While I may do some things well, waiting isn't one of them. And waiting on God to show up is the most painful place of waiting. At times, it has seemed to me as if

He has made a practice of showing up only some percentage of the time.

If you are anything like me, then you genuinely live as if you believe this to be God's track record. The reality is that we have been perfectly cared for throughout our lives. It has often been on a different time frame than our own and in very different ways. The house is too small, the car won't hold all those car seats, and the dad surely doesn't have what it takes to parent all those little lives. The truth of the matter is that we really do have what it takes and exactly nothing to offer. You are more than a breadwinner and a sperm donor.

We as men are equipped with everything we need to love our children well . . . and to fail them. Because the Spirit of God is alive in us, we are promised that we have the power of heaven at our disposal. Wouldn't you say your family is better than okay in light of that promise? However, the anchor is the flesh. The competition taking place between flesh and Spirit creates a perfect context for pain and disappointment to take place. But the reality is that God's greater purpose is our sanctification, not our purposes or even our enjoyment.

So, the house may be way too small for your liking and exactly the right size. There is something larger at play that requires waiting and listening . . . waiting on God to show up in a way that is at times familiar and comfortable and is at other times not.

Sleeping Through The Night

Never before has a good night's sleep seemed so wonderful and so unattainable. Despite what other parents (or books) may tell you, there is no magical age or method for making your baby sleep a full six to eight hours at night, as much as you might wish it would happen.

During their first few weeks, most babies sleep only about four hours at a time due to hunger. From three to six months, most babies begin to sleep more regularly, go to sleep more easily, and stay asleep longer.

However, you will never return to the days of being as fully rested as you were before children. Just about the time you think they have this sleep thing figured out, they'll surprise you. There will be illnesses, practicing newly learned skills at 2 a.m., teething, bad dreams, curfews, worrying, and many other things that will interrupt your sleep almost interminably. It's best to get used to those dark circles and bloodshot eyes. You will be tired for the next eighteen years.

So, what can you do to help them sleep (and you, too)? There are hundreds of different opinions, and you and your wife need to explore your philosophies together. Will you let the baby cry or not? What about allowing the baby or young child the opportunity of sleeping in the family bed? Is it okay to rock the baby to sleep, or should she be in her crib when she drifts off? Here are some fairly universal ideas:

• Establish a bed time routine which signals to your baby that it is time to wind down.

• When the baby needs care during the night, keep the lights dim and speak softly.

• Learn your baby's temperament and know that it will affect his sleep habits.

Although you're exhausted, when you look back at these months of late-night visits, you really will miss holding your baby in the wee hours of the morning. So, enjoy the gazing, cuddling, kissing, burping, cooing, and feeding. It won't last long.

"THE GREATNESS OF A MAN'S POWER IS THE MEASURE OF HIS SURRENDER."

—WILLIAM BOOTH

CHAPTER 8
WHAT IF SOMETHING TERRIBLE HAPPENS TO MY CHILD?

Duck. Duck. Duck. Goose! My (David) daughter exploded into the house and couldn't wait to tell me the news. Not only did she get to play Duck, Duck, Goose that day, but also, she had been chosen more than anyone else in the circle. She was three at the time and magically unaware that being chosen most often in the game of Duck, Duck, Goose doesn't equate to being the best player in the game. She had been a half step behind in developing her gross motor skills and was clearly not the fastest runner in the pack.

I can well remember playing the game as a child myself and searching out the slowest girl in the circle to make certain I made it safely to the empty spot without being tagged. Now my little girl was the "chosen one." I celebrated with her, as she was obviously ecstatic to share this news. I held back my sadness and was grateful that day for her lack of awareness. I dreaded the day when she would become painfully aware of her place in the pack.

I well remember discovering my place in the pack. I was one of the smallest boys in my grade, the shortest boy on the basketball team, and the smallest guy in the class. It was my story for many years. The biggest, most overweight kid in my class got nicknamed "The Jolly, Green Giant." Do you remember the Giant's sidekick on the vegetable cans? In case you don't remember that ad campaign, he was a little sprig of broccoli named "Sprout." That name would follow me right into the sixth grade yearbook. I hate that brand of vegetables to this day.

....

I remember begging God to make me grow. I even asked my parents to have me stretched. They would never agree to it. Most adolescent boys will hit some sort of physical growth spurt by at least eighth grade. Not me. I was three quarters into my freshman year of high school before my prayers were answered. The problem was that I forgot to ask God to make certain that my weight increased in proportion to my height. I was sure He would have known to do that on His own. He did not. I went from being the smallest guy in the class to the tallest, skinniest, and lankiest adolescent you would hate to encounter. How did this happen? I received exactly what I had been begging for so many years. That little sprig of broccoli turned into a long, tall, skinny green bean.

Now I have the opportunity to walk my own children through their journeys of childhood and adolescence. I have a lot of fear around that journey. I don't look forward to any seasons of life that involve introducing my kids to pain and disappointment. I cringe when I think about wiping my daughter's tears the first time she feels rejected by a boy. I dread sitting with my sons after not being chosen for a team, even though I know and believe, with everything in me, that it will make them strong, resilient, courageous, and compassionate. I know it is essential to their journey and part of sharing in the suffering of Christ. I understand all of that, and yet I want to resist it with every-thing in me.

Being a Christian offers no guarantee that your child will remain safe, secure, happy, or whole. As Dan Allender points out in *How Children Raise Parents*, "Not only does the Bible fail to provide a comprehensive guide to parenting, but it also fails to promise that if you follow the rules, your kids will turn out well." We can keep our children in Sunday School and then youth group until they turn eighteen, and the kids can still screw up.

In fact, we will go even further: Living in authentic relationship with Jesus actually brings more tension, chaos, and uncertainty to your life as a father. The more we know God and know ourselves, the more we come to realize how very little in control we really are. One of the deepest realities of authentic spirituality is the heartfelt awareness that "I am powerless." This is nowhere more true than in the category of parenting.

I (Stephen) have some close friends, Zach and Rebecca, who recently found out they were pregnant with their second child. It was glorious and surprising news. In order to conceive their first child, they spent thousands of dollars, endured months of invasive fertility procedures, offered years of prayer, and experienced "death" every month for two years. They eventually reached a point where they came to a loss of language to even talk about what they were experiencing or why. Zach and Rebecca had just begun a conversation about wanting a second child and did not expect to be able to get pregnant without medical intervention. They had decided to go back to the doctor in the next few months. But this time, no such effort was needed. Just, "Shazam! You're pregnant."

Imagine how amazed they were when one month, she missed her period and took a home pregnancy test that came out positive. Zach chose not to be present for the taking of the test, as it was too reminiscent of the many "deaths" he had experienced the first time around. They were ecstatic and stunned.

When I was with him next, he looked at me with a wry smile and, in his typical low key way, reported that his wife was pregnant. This was really early in the process, and he was still pretty blown away by the unexpected news. As we talked, he shared how astonished and thrilled he and

Rebecca both were. While extremely grateful, Zach was even more shocked. "What the @#$% is God thinking?" I remember him quipping.

The weeks that followed brought an increasing acceptance and excitement, as Zach and Rebecca continued to get their heads around the news. They told everyone they knew. A few weeks later, Zach and I had a telephone meeting scheduled for a Thursday afternoon. When I woke up that morning, however, Zach had left me a message on my voice mail saying he would be out of the office and needed to reschedule our appointment. "I'm at home. Call me when you get this," his message ended. (Besides being one of my most trusted friends, he is also a colleague.) He sounded in pain, breathless, and deflated, like someone had hit him in the gut and knocked the wind out of him. I called back as soon as I got his message. He answered the phone. After greeting each other, Zach said, "Rebecca has miscarried."

"When?" I asked.

"Yesterday," he replied.

Our conversation was short that day. The shock of being pregnant had not yet worn off when they were ambushed with this sad loss. In the weeks that followed Rebecca's miscarriage, Zach and Rebecca's hearts openly faced the ambivalence. Zach asked again, "What the @#$% is God doing?"—this time with more anger, awe, and humility. Rebecca wondered, "If we're not supposed to have a baby just now, why couldn't we just not be pregnant in the first place?"

What the @#$% is God doing, indeed? my heart raged. Through the process, I was humbled by Zach's gentleness and faith. *How could any good come of this?* I thought to myself. (I am amazed at how my faith can be so abiding one moment and how the next, I distrust God so blatantly.)

As I write, this chapter in Zach and Rebecca's lives is unresolved, as her body works to repair and heal from the trauma it has experienced. "What's God doing?" How can anyone know for sure? I suspect for Zach, this will be a time when his faith becomes more simple, and for Rebecca, a time when her faith becomes more complex. They have loyal, loving friends, and they are surrounded by a community of people who love them deeply. Because of their faith, they will be okay. And because of their faith, their hearts will ache all the more.

Failure, Pain, and Powerlessness

Guilt, heartache, and impotence are essential elements of biblical parenting. No matter how well-intentioned we are as dads, we will fail our children. Our mistakes as fathers will be physical. (I, Stephen, once dropped my daughter on her head in Target.) Our offenses will be emotional. (I snapped at my infant son who wouldn't let me sleep past 5:00 a.m.) Our transgressions will be psychological. (No matter how hard I try, I cannot be as consistent as I would like to be with my children.) Our sins will be spiritual. (All of the above.) Every day of our lives, we will fail our children. This will cause them and us heartache. (Sadly, most days, we will do it more than once.) And the raw truth is, we are powerless to stop it.

No matter how many books you read (and believe us, we've read almost all of them), no matter how many years of school you have, no matter how much experience you obtain, no matter how much (or how little) money you have, you cannot escape the reality that you will hurt your child—sometimes superficially, but sometimes the gash will be so deep that it may never fully heal in this life. Life is full of pain. And the majority of our children's pain will come from the hands, heart, and head of us as parents.

So what is a biblical response for fathers to failure, pain, and powerlessness? Lament. What is lament? Lament means to feel, show, and express grief. And grief more specifically is a combination of sadness, hurt, anger, fear, and loneliness. Time after time, the work of God is seen following the petition of the griever. Three biblical characters show us great examples of how to do lament really well: David, Job, and Jesus.

David as a king knew a lot about crying out to God. Time and time again, he would mourn, and God would respond. "I am trapped, please free me." "I have murdered, please forgive me." "I have doubted, please protect me." Here is an excerpt from Psalm 51, in which David writes regarding the moment of repentance after he had committed adultery with Bathsheba.

> Have mercy on me, O God,
> because of your unfailing love.
> Because of your great compassion,
> blot out the stain of my sins. . . .
> For I recognize my shameful deeds—
> they haunt me day and night.
> Against you, and you alone, have I sinned;
> I have done what is evil in your sight.
> You will be proved right in what you say,
> and your judgment against me is just.
> For I was born a sinner—
> yes, from the moment my mother conceived me.
> But you desire honesty from the heart,
> so you can teach me to be wise in my inmost being. . . .
> You would not be pleased with sacrifices,
> or I would bring them.

If I brought you a burnt offering,
you would not accept it.
The sacrifice you want is a broken spirit.
A broken and repentant heart, O God,
you will not despise.

David's adultery and murder had caused him great guilt and shame. He struggled with his own humiliation as a king, his failure as a man, and the evil in his own heart. He brought to God, through his lament, the only offering he had that was worthy: his broken heart.

Job, on the other hand, was one unfortunate dude. In the span of a few chapters, he loses his family, his health, and all his possessions. Job's response when all that he held dear was stripped from his life was to cry out to God in his own defense.

Then Job spoke again:
"My complaint today is still a bitter one, and I try hard not to groan aloud. If only I knew where to find God, I would go to his throne and talk with him there. I would lie out my case and present my arguments . . .
"I go east, but he is not there. I go west, but I cannot find him. I do not see him in the north, for he is hidden. I turn to the south, but I cannot find him. But he knows where I am going. And when he has tested me like gold in a fire, he will pronounce me innocent.
"For I have stayed in God's paths; I have followed his ways and not turned aside. I have not departed from his commands but have treasured his word in my heart. Nevertheless, his mind concerning me remains unchanged, and who can turn him from

his purposes? Whatever he wants to do, he does. So he will do for me all he has planned. He controls my destiny. No wonder I am so terrified in his presence. When I think of it, terror grips me. God has made my heart faint; the Almighty has terrified me. Darkness is all around me; thick, impenetrable darkness is everywhere." (Job 23:1-17, NLT)

Job knew heartache and fear, and he also knew his God. He was scared and hurt and undoubtedly a little ticked off. Job was experiencing one of the brutal realities of biblical faith: Following God means you suffer more than unbelievers, and in that suffering, we discover new things about ourselves.

Jesus knew lament, too—especially on the cross. Right before His death, when the agony was the greatest, His body bloodied and broken, and hope was slipping, He cried out to God in sorrow and loneliness:

> Then, at that time Jesus called out with a loud voice, "Eloi, Eloi, lema sabachthani?" which means, "My God, my God, why have you forsaken me?" (Mark 15:34, NLT)

In His sorrow, Jesus was referencing poetry of David from Ps. 22:1-2 (NLT).

> My God, my God! Why have you forsaken me?
> Why do you remain so distant?
> Why do you ignore my cries for help?
> Every day I call to you, my God,
> but you do not answer.
> Every night you hear my voice,
> but I find no relief.

Surely the Jews in the crowd would have known this, just as they would have known how the Psalm continues.

> But I am a worm and not a man.
> I am scorned and despised by all! . . .
> Yet you brought me safely from my mother's womb
> and led me to trust you when I was a nursing infant.
> I was thrust upon you at my birth.
> You have been my God from the moment I was born.
> Do not stay so far from me,
> for trouble is near,
> and no one else can help me.

As Jesus demonstrates, lament is not an absence of faith; it is an exercise of relationship. It is an opportunity to cry out to a God who at times doesn't feel real and remember who He is and who He has been. Lament is movement toward surrender to our powerlessness. Jesus' final words were a declaration of surrender to the reality that as a broken man, He was powerless. There was no other way out except through the cross.

The common theme in all three of these examples is suffering. None of these people lived life in an effort to avoid suffering. In the case of David, his suffering is for the most part due to his disobedience. For Job, his suffering comes at the hand of God by way of the devil. For Christ, suffering is a consequence of loving well. As Eugene Peterson points out in his introduction to Job in The Message Remix: The Bible in Contemporary Language, "One of the surprises as we get older, however, is that we come to see that there is no real correlation between the amount of wrong we commit and the pain we experience." Peterson continues, "An even larger surprise is that very often there is something quite the opposite."

The lesson is that no matter what we do, pain will come, and if we let it, it can be our teacher. As fathers, God will use our tears to cleanse our hearts, stained black by sin, so that they glisten to reflect His image. As parents, it is not until we have a crisis of character (like David, Job, or Jesus) that we will have the opportunity to step into surrendering the safety and security of our child to the care of God. For some of us, this happens early in the process (like pregnancy or birth); for others, this happens when our children hit middle school or high school or college: a pregnant daughter, an addicted son, a critically injured teenager, a terminally ill prom queen.

In order for us to be the man and father God longs for us to be, He is willing to do whatever it takes on our behalf. That's how crazy He is for each of us. His promise is to love us and restore us and redeem our hearts and bodies to their intended glory. But so much of our redemption as fathers is going to depend on how much suffering we are committed to enduring on behalf of our children.

He will comfort us, but He will never coddle us. He will engage us, but He will never manipulate us. He will provide for us more than what we ever could dream of, but He will never overindulge us. And whether we like it or not (I surely don't), maturity of the heart is synonymous with failure, pain, and powerlessness.

GREAT RISK AND GREAT REWARD

I (David) remember being in our OBGYN's office eight months into our second pregnancy. We had received the news that we were carrying twins midway through the pregnancy. Our doctor had already gone over the list of possibilities involved with a high-risk pregnancy. We had taken a class on birthing multiples and explored many of the common complications in delivery. Even with that information, we weren't prepared to hear our doctor say that the amniotic fluid was low with my first son. The doctor was recommending we induce immediately to reduce risk for Baby A. Baby B had been identified as smaller and needing additional time to continue his development. Reducing risk for one son would require increasing the risk for another. I never wanted to have to make that kind of decision. We prayerfully agreed to the induction and prepared to go into the hospital. I remember thinking, *What if something terrible happens?* It felt like gambling to me. I found peace only in knowing God had formed both of those lives from the first moments, and He was sovereign.

We also had the gift of a gracious and skilled physician with whom we had developed a rich connection. I was thankful for his discernment, guidance, and experience. We experienced several critical moments during our delivery, but my sons are safely in this world, and I am so grateful for that.

However, I have walked with several close friends whose stories do not mirror mine. We know multiple couples with whom we have grieved over miscarriages. We have also shared in the burial of a young child with some dear and precious friends. It is deep and intense sadness. It is mystery that I do not claim to understand. What I have experienced through my own journey and the shared journey of friends is that at some point, we encounter an opportunity to surrender. When I encounter tragedy, I believe there is a great tendency in me to want to pull back or separate myself out from the possibilities or the realities. If there is a chance that the pain will involve loss or death, I want to refrain from investing myself completely. In a moment following our OBGYN appointment, I had the thought, *It would surely be easier to lose a son I had not yet met than one I had known and loved.* It was a foolish thought and a fruitless effort to save myself from the intensity of loss—something I could never fully do.

The truth is that if I had never seen my son Witt take a single breath, I knew him because I had dreamed of who he would be. I had imagined in my mind, from the moment the ultrasound revealed his gender—what he would look like and how it would be to have a son. My wife and I had named him and knew each of my twin sons before she delivered them into this world. He was my son from the moment he was first formed inside my wife's body.

I cannot escape the experience of knowing him and loving him. I attempted to separate myself from it for a moment when I didn't know if he would be alive when I met him. I reached a fork in the road. One was the road of surrender. There was no guarantee that we would leave the delivery room with two infants. What if we made the wrong decision? What if the risk we diminished created a greater risk than we had imagined? What if something terrible happens? The road of surrender is full of mystery and questions. There is so much unknown. I relinquish much in traveling this direction. This road may involve experiencing deep sadness and loss. I often travel with only hope and obedience. It often involves waiting.

Control is an illusion, really. This road will end at some point, as all roads eventually do. Reaching the end involves remembering. As men, we often want the road of distraction. We see this effort every day in our work. As men, we are champions at this effort. We go to great lengths to avoid pain. We go to really destructive places in our attempts. We run to media, pornography, substances, food, sports, work, other relationships, and many other places. It is a futile attempt.

Perhaps there is confusion and uncertainty surrounding your experience in parenting right now. It may have come in the form of miscarriage or may be news of a high risk pregnancy. Possibly you are dealing with physical or emotional challenges with your child. The question becomes, "Will I allow myself to love this child, or will I hold back for fear that something will go wrong?" If this is your story, you are in the midst of a calling to surrender, an invitation to press in to whatever comes next. It may be deep joy or intense loss. Whatever it is, we hope you will move into mystery. The fear of losing one of my sons could have kept me absent in the delivery room. I wanted to be present then, and I want to be present now.

TRAGEDY

Will something terrible happen to your child? Probably at some point. For some of us, that "terrible" will be more severe than for others. The greater question is, how will you prepare your child to engage the suffering that will most certainly come? To do that requires that you face the same question in your own life.

Do you fundamentally believe that God loves your child more than you do? If you dare, it will have profound implications in your life and how your father. It will free you to risk your child's happiness, security, and safety in the hopes of him/her living fully.

God designed parenting as a place where people can come to ask hard questions, engage deep heartache, and find renewed hope—a place people can grow in the range and richness of new possibility in their lives. It is a place where people can step into the process of maturity of heart and discover that living fully means more than happiness, comfort, or thrills—it means having the capacity to experience true joy, yet being equally capable of grieving to the depths while holding on to hope.

Eventually, if we as fathers desire to live authentically and biblically, we must turn the care of our children over to the only Father with enough love and power to secure their future. This is arguably the most difficult act we will do as fathers—surrendering our child to another—The Other. To do this takes a faith not born from rituals, tradition, or cultural expectations, but rather a faith that deeply abides in the hope of the resurrected and returning Jesus. It is in only this kind of intimate relationship with God that we can truly love our sons and daughters well. The great reward comes in realizing that as I surrender my heart and my child's heart more to the care of God, I grow stronger and wiser and kinder and more authentic in the process.

Uncovering a Father's Heart

So why all this rigmarole? Why does the Father allow pain, suffering, and sorrow? The express purpose of suffering in the masculine heart is to draw us close to God and refine our character as fathers. Suffering drives us to powerlessness, neediness, and vulnerability. The masculine heart is often tough and calloused. God longs for our heart to be tender and passionate, so that when we offer it to our children, it is useful to them.

In my (Stephen) backyard, I have a walnut tree that bears a lot of fruit. Every now and then, I walk through the yard with my toddler-aged son looking for nuts. When we find one, he screams, "WALNUT, DADDY!" which is my cue to pick it up and hurl it across the yard at a large hackberry tree toward the back of our lot. If I hit the tree, he erupts in delight. "Again!" he demands. "Again! More walnuts!" he exclaims, pronouncing walnut as two distinct words: wall nut.

What only my son and I know is that somewhere between the time he yells, "Walnut!" and the time the nut smashes into the tree, I become a Major League Baseball pitcher. Sometimes I'm Gregg Maddox. Other times I am Roger Clemens. Occasionally I am Nolan Ryan.

It struck me the other day that the male heart is a lot like one of these walnuts. On the outside is a thick husk (or male ego). This is a thick, yellow-green skin. Beneath the husk is black slime. In our hearts, this grit is the residue of years of guilt and shame. This black silt covers the hard shell of the nut and stains whatever it comes into contact with. Smooth and grooved, this casing hidden by the black rot is nearly impenetrable. Formed by harm and fear, this shell is made to protect the valuable fruit of the human heart.

To put it bluntly, God is a glorious nutcracker. (We mean that in every sense of the word.) If it seems that God is out to bust your shell, you're right. Much of life before and after becoming a believer is about being exposed as desperately needy. God is passionately interested in ridding our hearts of the layers of husk, slime, and shell that encase our souls in darkness. And His chief tool? Pain.

Loss of some kind or another always precedes brokenness, brokenness always precedes surrender, and surrender always precedes sanctification. So if God is in the business of sanctifying our hearts, then key parts of that experience are loss, brokenness, and surrender. If you haven't figured it out yet, you soon will: Parenting is full of failure (yours, your wife's, and your kids'). At any given moment in my (Stephen's) family, somebody is doing something that falls short of glorifying God. Occasionally this is my wife. Sometimes it's my kids. Frequently it's me.

As a parent, I let my own willfulness, determination, ambitions, and agendas come between what I know to be right and what I end up doing. As hard as I try, and as much as I hate that it's true, I often fail as a father. God is much less concerned with what I do (my behavior) than He is with who I am (my character).

If you have only the smallest amount of love for your child, then the weight of parenting will be too much for you to bear. The responsibility of growing this child in the image of God is overbearing. You cannot do it alone. If you try, you will certainly fail. At best, parenting will uncover your powerlessness and drive you before the throne of grace. At worst, you will commit to self-sufficiency, or you will back out of the game and abdicate your role as father to your wife, or the school, or the Church.

The only power you and I have is to refuse God—to turn our backs on His love. We don't even have the power to really choose Him. He has already chosen us. The same is true with our children. They already love us. The heart of a child has to endure incredible amounts of trauma, abuse, and abandonment in order for the love he or she feels for his or her father to diminish. So the decision we must make in the early stages of fatherhood is, (1) Will I allow myself to love this child with all that I am (even though that certainly means failing)? or (2) Will I hold back in order to protect my own fragile ego? If we step into the game and say, "Yes!" to love, we will discover that God will do for us what we cannot do for ourselves—love our children well.

WHAT IF SOMETHING TERRIBLE HAPPENS …?

135

Choosing A Pediatrician

If you have read any other books about becoming a parent, you have probably seen lists of questions to consider as you choose a pediatrician. You might even be thinking, *What's the big deal?* However, before your child's second birthday, you (and/or your wife) will likely have spent more hours in the pediatrician's office than you want to remember! So this decision is an important one.

Beyond the practical questions that many parenting books enumerate, what do you and your wife need to discuss and agree on during this process? Here are a few things to consider:

• How involved will you be in doctor visits? Will your schedule allow you to go to appointments, or will your wife be the main liaison with the doctor?

• What is more important to you in pediatric care: a connection with the doctor, or his or her credentials?

• Is the sex of your child a factor in choosing a pediatrician? For example, are you comfortable having your daughter see a male pediatrician?

• Do you prefer to have a pediatrician who is also a parent? Are you able to trust the recommendations of a childless doctor, or do you prefer someone who has personal experience in dealing with sleepless nights, sick children, temper tantrums, and other problems you will face?

• Finally, be sure to look at the entire practice of the pediatrician. In group practices, you may often see other doctors. In large practices, believe it or not, there is often a nurse on call twenty-four hours a day, seven days a week. This may not seem like a big deal now, but when your sweet angel is screaming at 3 a.m. with a fever of 102° F, it sure is nice to talk to someone who knows what they're talking about!

> "**T**HE BEST WAY TO PREPARE
> IS TO BEGIN TO LIVE."
>
> —ELLIOT HUBBORD

CHAPTER NINE
How Do I Prepare?

I (Stephen) remember being in the delivery room with my wife when our first child was born. As the doctor announced the arrival of this creature, she flipped our newborn upside-down, its rear end facing my wife and me. "Here you go! Congratulations!" the doctor proclaimed. I remember thinking something like, *Here is what? What am I looking at?* It wasn't until my wife explained, "It's a girl!" that it hit me what was staring me in the face. Many times since that first encounter with my daughter, I have had those same feelings of uncertainty and confusion— bound by a nagging feeling that I should know more than I really do.

A few days later, I was standing over my daughter as she was sleeping in her crib. I was in shock. I didn't really know what to do. I had a vague sense of it, but the reality of the moment was still really foggy. I wasn't ready. I hadn't finished the few books I bought. I went to as many classes that the hospital provided, but I still wasn't ready for this moment. Then, like something out of a movie, I saw her future roll out before me: her first day of school, her first soccer game, her prom, her high school graduation, her first job, her wedding, her children. Questions exploded in my head: How did I get here? What do I do now? How do I begin to move forward? What is this parenting thing all about?

By this point in the book, you probably have picked up on the idea that we think being a father is really important— both for the man and the child. Throughout this book, we have pressed hard into the concept that this season in a man's life is a divine invitation into fuller manhood and more authentic living. Fatherhood is a right of passage loaded with moments you can never have back.

How will you get ready to live through them? Will you do what it takes to be present to all of the sights, sounds, smells, and feelings of it all, or will you choose just to move through life numb? While there will be many days you will choose the latter, our hope is that you will opt for "presence." Every moment with your wife or child is an opportunity for you to engage in the process: a process that calls forth creativity, passion, pain, and mystery.

If you are anything like us, you will probably fail more often than you succeed, but how sweet it is when we stumble into success. Get used to falling down. Parenthood is a dimly lit, rough path with many rocks along the trail. If you are living in it well, you will never fully feel competent, confident, or secure.

In order to help you better find your way as you traverse this brave new world, this chapter addresses some commonly quoted verses, as well as briefly explores some biblical categories to help you begin to develop your own framework for what fathering can look like generally as parents and more specifically as a father.

What's Biblical About Parenting?

A friend quipped to me (Stephen) the other day, "Parenting is God's payback for the Garden." While not altogether theologically accurate, sometimes I agree. There are times in my life, as a father of young children, that I am amazed how soon deception and self-centeredness are expressed by my kids. Like, when my toddler son is rolling on the floor because he can't watch another episode of

Veggie Tales. Or when my preschool daughter asks me for permission to do something, I say, "No," and then minutes later, I hear her in the next room asking her mother. Or when after an extremely long day with sleep on the horizon and my wife at the movies, neither child will go to sleep. Surely, I reason, "God has it out for me."

Since becoming a father, I have learned more about God's relationship with me than I ever knew possible. I've glimpsed the extent of His patience with me (through my impatience with my own children). I've tasted the grief He must feel when He sees His children choose folly over wisdom. I've sampled His frustration when my kids pass up on my love just to have it their own way. Unlike God, my own pride, self-centeredness, and fatigue direct far too much of my interactions with my children, but even with that reality, kids can be hard to be with—let alone parent.

Then there are those times when a get I whiff of heaven: a walk holding my daughter's hand; the hardy laugh of my son when I tickle him; a wrestling match on the floor with my kids; the press of cold toddler feet into my stomach as we snuggle in bed on a Saturday morning; the golden setting sun illuminating my daughter's face on a summer evening. These moments, too, are opportunities for me to hold, if only for an instant, a measure of the weight of God's love for me.

Being a father has exposed me to God's immense love of me. There will be times when I am overwhelmed with the realization that all the richness of love I have for my children is meager in comparison to how extravagantly God loves me. There is no way you or I will ever live up to His degree of favor. He wants so much more for us than we could ever want for ourselves. I didn't really understand that until I had children.

A Framework for Fathering

As men, we need to contend with who we can be as fathers. If we hope to father well, we must wrestle with questions like:

- What am I to do with and for my children?
- What goals do I have as a father?
- What tactics should I employ to achieve my goals?

These are complex and worthy questions that need to be asked if we are going to succeed as fathers. But as disciples of Jesus, our call to fatherhood transcends even these important questions. As Christian fathers, we must grapple with issues like glory and evil, dignity and depravity, heaven and hell. As believers in the resurrection, fathering invokes much deeper questions, such as:

- How do we father in ways that help usher in the kingdom of heaven?
- How does my own sanctification come into play in my parenting?
- How is God interacting in my life through my child?
- Will I let my relationship with my God affect how I engage my child? If so, how?

We follow a God who is committed to engaging each of us on intensely personal levels. How He intersects one man's life may be very different from how He intersects another's. While we men may share similarities in our stories, the details are very personal. The God of Creation is a God of detail—it is always in the details that we will find the fingerprints of God. So any framework we can provide must only be the foundation for a biblical worldview of fatherhood. For example, God is at play in your life through the Spirit. Generally, this is for His glory through your sanctification, but how you reveal His glory is vastly different than anyone else. We are each unique image bearers, and for that reason, we will each be His unique in how God intends us to father. You must do the work in relationship with God to discover what He intends for you as a father, who you are to be as a father, and what you are to do as a father. All that being said, we believe that there are some broad biblical categories and approaches that can serve to help you undergird a personal approach to fathering. While not entirely comprehensive, we believe these three main categories are a great place to begin: (1) Character, (2) Scripture, and (3) Relationship.

CHARACTER

While there are many extraordinary personalities in Scripture useful for developing a perspective of fatherhood, any biblical model must include as its foundation our Triune God. Each component of the Trinity has implications for how we father. If we try to weave these characteristics into our work as fathers, we will be well down the road to providing a taste of relationship with God for our children. To do this for each head of the Trinity, we need to ask:

1) What implications does this have on fathering?
2) What characteristics uniquely define this part of God?

Father is perhaps the most often used metonym for God. We see a lot of our relationship with our Heavenly Creator through this window. While infrequent in the Old Testament, reading the Gospels and Epistles and other

New Testament texts shows us that much of what Jesus did in His ministry from a theological perspective was to deconstruct, disrupt, and expand the prevailing view of God by emphasizing the picture of God as "father." In this, Christ paints a picture of a God who is defined by three primary characteristics: interpersonal (He relates one on one), interactive (He is responsive), and proactive (He has a plan). Working out these categories gives us some great boundaries to play within as fathers. Throughout the New Testament, we also see God the Father as ruler, provider, and judge. As this King/Father, He rules by orchestrating opportunities for individuals' redemption, providing a context for personal transformation, and shaping and teaching us how to live through discipline. As you look to weave an image of the Father into your framework, you must consider what it looks like for you to be like God the Father:

- interpersonal (you must engage your child one on one),
- interactive (you need to be responsive to his/her needs and desires), and
- proactive (you cannot wait for him/her to make the first move).

God as Son also includes a matrix of categories that begin to fill out the experience of the Trinity in our lives as fathers. Three of the ways Jesus lived out His divinity was as a sacrifice, a teacher, and a real-life example. First and foremost, Christ was the atonement for our sins—the perfect offering who suffered and died on our behalf so we can live (both now and forever). He was willing to do for you and me what no one else could/would do. In that way, sacrifice for our children is an essential element of biblical fathering.

Like Christ, fathers are to lovingly and wisely sacrifice themselves on behalf of their children. Stated differently, fathers must be willing to ache and suffer on behalf of their children. To the extent we are willing to grieve with and for our children, they will see Christ in us and experience Christ alive in their own stories.

As a teacher, the Son illuminated the truth of God in ways that were invitational and transformative. As dads, we are uniquely positioned to reveal the reality of God in an ugly world so that our children can respond to the truth that is within them. Beyond teacher, however, Jesus "walked the walk" for us. In doing so, He not only prepared a path, He also gave us an example to follow for how to lead, love, and serve. This is directly tied to how we must father. If you want to know how to father, study the life and relationships of Jesus.

The third leg of the Trinity, the Spirit, cannot go overlooked if we hope to offer a biblically accurate framework modeled on God. The work of the Spirit is to come alongside, comfort, and heal. This is an area where many fathers fail to find ways to support and engage their children. It is sometimes hard for us men to move from the teacher to the helper/healer. There will be times in your child's life when teaching them is inappropriate and even harmful. An example: No kid wants to be showed the proper technique for riding her bike when she has just flipped over the handlebars. Or when your son doesn't make varsity, one of the worst things you could do is make it a teaching moment. What he needs more than anything is an arm around his shoulders helping him grieve his losses.

The topic of character, as the basic level in the framework of biblical fatherhood, is modeled on these seven characteristics of the Holy Trinity:

- interpersonal
- interactive
- proactive
- sacrificial
- teacher
- model
- helper/healer

SCRIPTURE

A second component to a biblical fathering framework is submission to Scripture. The trouble is, like everything else in life, Scripture does not say a whole lot on the specific dos and don'ts of fathering. It does provide, however, some general categories for us as dads, and when it comes to parenting, maybe the most frequently quoted Scriptures are:

- "He who spares the rod hates his son." (Prov. 13:24a)
- "Train a child in the way he should go, and when he is old he will not turn from it." (Prov. 22:6)

These are also perhaps two of the most misquoted Scriptures attached to being a father (or mother). Accurately, the focus of these two verses is parenting, but their meanings are often bent far from the context of the text. When taken in context of the text, they become a great place to begin a biblical theology for parenting.

To do so, it might help to first talk a little about the genre of "proverb." Proverbs are not unique to Christianity or Judaism. They are common among many faith traditions and philosophies, such as Buddhism, Hinduism, and Islam. Even Ben Franklin wrote proverbs. "A penny saved is a penny earned," would be one extra-biblical example.

Whether biblically oriented or not, all proverbs have a similar structure. Proverbs serve more as mini-life lessons than they do as success formulas. Proverbs should not be read as a causal, "If you don't do 'X,' then 'Y' will happen," but rather as pieces of ancient wisdom principles handed down from one generation to another. Scripture confirms this. Other biblical wisdom texts like Job and Ecclesiastes make it clear that there are no secret formulas for Christian success and happiness.

To Rod or Not to Rod

So how do these two proverbs prepare us as fathers? Let's start with Prov. 13:24 (NLT). It reads, "He who spares the rod hates his son . . . but he who loves him is careful to discipline him." Often Prov. 13:24 is used to advocate corporal punishment—using physical pain as a penalty for sin and deterrent for future behavior (usually spanking). In fact, the book of Proverbs is full of similarly direct verses.

- "Discipline your son, for in that there is hope; do not be a willing party to his death." (19:18)
- "Folly is bound up in the heart of the child, but the rod of discipline will drive it far from him." (22:15)
- "Do not withhold discipline from your child; if you punish him with the rod, he will not die. Punish him with the rod and save his soul from death." (23:13-14)
- "The rod of correction imparts wisdom, but a child left to himself disgraces his mother." (29:15)
- "Discipline your son and he will give you peace; he will bring delight to your soul." (29:17)

While references to "the rod" cannot be overlooked (it's mentioned in four of these five verses), is spanking really the point? Are the Proverbs making a biblical injunction to spank our children? Probably not. At a closer read, these verses seem to be saying less about "the rod" and more about the inward attitude and calling of the parent. More simply put,

- How is a parent to be? and
- What are parents to do?

The emphasis of "the rod" proverbs could be summed up with something like, "Lovingly discipline your children with wisdom, so that when they are grown, they may be wise." Or stated conversely, "If you aren't loving and wise with discipline, your children will be fools." The mandate for parents is to be wise and loving, not necessarily to spank your child. These proverbs are directed toward the heart of parents, not their mode of discipline. At this level, the level of the heart, "the rod" is a technique, a vehicle for delivering the instruction, not the instruction itself. The point is love and wisdom, not "the rod." Peterson's Message translates Proverbs 13:24 this way: "A refusal to correct is a refusal to love; love your children by disciplining them."

TRAINING DAYS

"Train a child in the way he should go, and when he is old he will not turn from it" (Proverbs 22:6). Many people have misinterpreted this proverb as well. It has often been taught as a warranty for happy, healthy, and secure children: "If you do all the right things, then your kids will do right when they are adults." Biblical parenting does not come with a money-back guarantee. You can be the best parent in the world and do everything perfectly, and your daughter will still fall short, struggle, suffer, and sin. You can raise your son in a church that is spiritually rich, relationally healthy, and culturally relevant, and you will not guarantee his salvation or sanctification. Any perspective that advocates this kind of theology runs contrary to the teachings of Scripture and subverts the true freedom inherent in the biblical story.

If this is not a secret formula for success, then what is this proverb saying to fathers? Let's focus on one phrase: "train a child." The entire verse hangs on these words. These three words are the launching pad to a series of important parenting questions and answers.

- Question: "Train him how?"
- Answer: "In the way he should go."
- Question: "Which way should he go?"
- Answer: "His way."

This pronoun, "his," is singular, implying that we are to parent very specifically for each child—address each child's unique bent. Let's explain. Ask any father with more than one child about how his children are different, and he will go on and on and on. Any successful coach knows that to maximize performance, you need to address and train each player's individual and specific needs. For instance, it would be foolish to parent a quiet, reserved, or shy child the same as you would an outgoing, rambunctious, or aggressive child. Every child is different, and to parent effectively, we must see the unique heart of each child. Isn't that how God approaches us—each in our own way?

From these two passages, the framework for a biblical theology of fathering begins to emerge even more clearly. Based on these two proverbs, at the very least, two things are required: 1) Fathers are to lovingly instill wisdom, and 2) Fathers are to address each child's unique heart.

Generally, as parents, our goal is to shepherd our child through life toward maturing her into how she was uniquely stamped in the image of God. To do this well requires that parents lovingly address their child's unique heart together in a manner that takes into account the unique qualities, callings, and sinfulness peculiar to that child (and each parent). This process of lovingly growing maturity takes place solely in the cauldron of interdependent relationships—namely between the parents (husband and wife), the parents and child, the parents and God, and the child and God.

The result is a paradoxical network of parenting relationships. Insomuch as godly mothering and godly fathering are similar and mutually dependent, whatever it means to effectively mother has little bearing on effective fathering (and vice versa). While successful parenting is indeed a co-labor between husband and wife, it is quite possible for a mother to be an exceptional mother while the father is a failure. (Or the father to do everything well and the mother be deficient.) Therefore, the first step in being an effective father or mother is to understand the unique and vital role you play in the life of your child (to grow his/her glory toward the likeness of God), and how you are equipped and hindered in living out that role.

How mothers and fathers perform in their roles as parents is dependent as much on their unique personhood as it is on the uniqueness of their individual child. Just as these relational styles influence all other relationships, these styles of relating dictate very much how fathers and mothers will parent together. However, it is possible (and helpful) to identify the general differences between mothers and fathers (or more accurately, how their differences as men and women affect their roles as parents).

Wisdom, Image Building, and Love

While parenting styles are not rooted solely in gender, they are greatly influenced by it, and therefore, placing the male/female differences in a context of parenting provides a helpful framework.

Godly fathering is to lovingly unveil and impart in a child those characteristics that are inherently male (namely strength and courage), according to how these characteristics are uniquely present in his child, in order to grow the glory of his child more toward the likeness of God.

Godly mothering is to lovingly grow and nurture in a child those characteristics that are inherently feminine (namely tenderness and beauty), according to how these characteristics are uniquely present in her child, in order to grow the glory of her child more toward the likeness of God.

As a man, you have the opportunity to uniquely reveal and reflect the love of God in your child's life. Of course, how you participate in doing this should differ based on your personality and your child's. There are, however, general categories that offer understanding when it comes to fathering.

Biology and Fatherhood

At the foundational level, a father is distinctly different from his children. Whereas a mother is organically linked to her children from the moment of conception; a father is not. Here is how: A mother secretes high doses of oxytocin, progesterone, and estrogen biochemicals that hormonally bond her offspring to her (she is the chemical host). This biological bonding even extends beyond the womb, as the mother continues to deliver the physical and emotional sustenance of life through breast feeding. As dads, we change the diapers, give baths, and put together the cribs. Consequently, as men, we do not have the rich biological attachment of mothers. We start off parenting behind the eight ball. As Michael Gurian stresses in *The Wonder of Girls*, "The male body requires greater reliance of both emotional and social bonding systems in order to complete the father's attachment to his offspring." We men are not biochemically bonded to our children in the same way as our wives. Emotionally, we must bond to our children through social systems of status, social pressure, marriage, protecting, providing, role modeling, and spirituality.

In our maleness, we are uniquely positioned to teach our children to handle the daily demands of life in a way that inspires strength and courage. This begins with our own personal courage and a willingness to craft an atmosphere in the home that does three things:

- fights male/female stereotypes,
- models emotional strength in the family, and
- creates a world that tolerates tension and mystery.

In deconstructing the stereotypes of male/female gender roles, while still encouraging each child's natural inclination, we can help instill in our sons and daughters a sense of adventure and courage that is not chained by the misogynistic structures of *Father Knows Best* or *The Brady Bunch*.

Secondly, when a father has enough maturity to be his own man, he allows his children to develop in healthy ways as individuals. Finally, fathers need to tolerate tension, conflict, and disagreement in the home. Conflict is a natural part of being in relationship, and if a father suppresses tension, he may find his children expressing their might and desire for liberty and justice in unhealthy ways. All three

of these struggles lead children toward independence and
strength and away from codependency on the father, other
family members, or peers.

FATHERING DAUGHTERS

Since leaving the Garden, God has given men a perplexing
biological challenge as fathers of daughters: "How do I
connect with something fundamentally other?" In the most
basic ways, our daughters don't look like us. As fathers,
this role of advocacy and king in our daughters' lives is
most played out in the core dynamic of sexuality. While
other prominent differences exist (such as age, culture,
life experience, genetics, worldview, and even race), the
broadest gap we must learn to bridge if we hope to impact
our daughters for good is sexuality. We are not bridging this
gap in an effort to overcome or negate the issue of sexuality,
but rather, the bridge becomes an avenue for relationship
between father and daughter so we can impact their lives,
and they ours. To adequately explore the father/daughter
relationship, we need to examine it from two perspectives.

- How does a daughter's unique sexual otherness from
  her father present challenges and opportunities for
  relationship, and how can his otherness from his
  daughter help each of them grow more fully into who
  they are each intended by God to be?
- What specific gifts can a father, in his maleness, bring
  to his daughter? In other words, how can he, in love,
  bring himself to receive his daughter fully?

There is something unequaled about the father/daughter
relationship. As Gurian points out, there is no way to
understate the importance of a father in a girl's life.

A girl must know, with all her big heart, that she is loved by her father. Regardless of his style of fathering, a man who supports his daughter's progress can become her oracle. He carries from his closeness with her an abiding—even if unconscious—sense of prediction about how his daughter will turn out.

A father plays a part in his daughter's life that no other person can. He is her advocate and king, always in action for her. If he is willing in his action to risk giving her his heart and receiving hers, then they both will benefit— him by seeing her grow into loveliness; her by gaining independence (strength) and an understanding about how that will enable her as a woman to risk loving others well (courage). She will know that she has value and beauty. She will understand that she has the capacity to uncover tenderness and beauty, as well as strength and courage, in others. If he is willing to suffer emotional pain on her behalf, a father will experience strength and value like he has never known.

In our culture, there are signs of erosion to the father/ daughter relationship. This erosion has caused a landslide of effect on girls. Here are some of the results to girls when they are raised without a substantial bond to their daddies. They are more likely to include:

- being sexually abused, molested, and raped
- experiencing other physical violence
- divorce late in life
- receiving lower grades in school
- being suspended or expelled
- experiencing child abuse and domestic violence
- having trouble with the police
- living in poverty and economic insecurity

- finding and staying in lower-paying jobs as adults
- bearing children while they are still children.[1]

In many ways, we teach our daughters more about their femininity than their mothers. Like looking in a mirror, we get a real sense of who we are by experiencing our opposite. It is a father's job to help his daughter accept herself as a woman without guilt or anxiety. As fathers, we must overcome our own shame of not being enough and learn to father from within our own giftedness: as creative, passionate beings willing to step into tension and mystery with courage and faith. If we do this with our daughters, they will embrace their sexuality without shame or fear.

In her book, *Reviving Ophelia*, Mary Pipher discusses how in her research, a father's "emotional availability . . . was the crucial variable" in the quality of the father/daughter relationship—not whether or not he lived in the home. This does not mean that we are void of a capacity to nurture, but simply that masculine nurturing looks different from feminine nurturing. For example, while a woman's nurturing may grow tenderness, as men, we need our nurturing to grow strength and courage.

Fathering Sons

Just as there is something specific that stirs in us through the experience of parenting daughters, something similar but very different can happen to us through parenting sons.

If the challenge of fathering a daughter comes in her fundamental difference, the difficulty in fathering a son comes in his "sameness." Our sons have the capacity to call us out—forcing us to face our own masculinity (or lack of it). Because he looks like us, the chances are he will be like us.

1. This list reflects the work of David Blackenhorn, who culled statistics and studies from the U.S. and other countries, as cited in *The Wonder of Girls* by Michael Gurian.

As dads, we reconnect with our own experience of being a boy and a son. We see ourselves. At times, we attempt to redeem our stories through our sons; other times, we are seeking to reinvent ourselves. Regardless of what direction we go in our experience of parenting boys or girls, it is important to understand our story . . . all of it.

I (David) have been working with boys in different counseling settings for over ten years now. There are some very specific things I have observed and experienced with boys that I believe require a unique vision for caring for them. For the last several years, I have been teaching a class on nurturing boys. I love the opportunity to dialogue with parents, grandparents, educators, mentors, youth directors, and other people who care for boys. A lot about boys is mysterious . . . who they are, what they need, how they learn, and what they want.

Boys tend to speak and sometimes act in code. It is at times difficult for them to articulate their experience well. What they feel can tend to come out sideways. There is a great deal of decoding that needs to take place in the process of caring for them. I encourage parents to think about the questions they are asking and the ones they aren't asking. Both questions are important and a window into the soul of a boy. We don't generally serve boys well when it comes to modeling for them what it looks like for emotions to be in the life of a man. This deficit, paired with their internal wiring, brings about much of the mystery we experience in seeking to understand them.

There are some foundational things I believe they need from us as fathers. They need, as previously mentioned, to see that emotions belong in the life of a man. They need our strength, and they need to experience that physically, emotionally, spiritually, and relationally. They need to feel like we are passionate about who they are and what they love. This can be a particular challenge for us as fathers if we find our sons love things that we don't love or are different from the things we know and enjoy.

Spirituality and Fatherhood

Culturally, the family is in shambles, and the art of fathering is on the decline. Family systems continue to break down. Secular researcher Rebekah Levine Coley points out in an article entitled "(In)visible Men" that as the economy shifted from agriculture toward industrialization, fathers transitioned from working from home with the family to laboring in factories. In the last century, as women moved from the home to the workforce, it increased women's financial freedom and made paternal financial support less necessary. This isn't all. Coley goes on to argue that these financial trends, coupled with other things, including declining fertility, increasing rates of divorce and remarriage, and heightened rates of non-marital childbearing, have contributed to the removal of many men from traditional fathering roles and often from their children's households, leading to complex family systems with unclearly defined roles for fathers.

Creating a context for Christ in the home is crucial in this imploding culture, where truth is relative and all experience is personal. Building an environment where our children can flee from us as parents and cling to God is critical and needs to be a father's priority. Ultimately, if we are going to be successful as fathers, it is imperative that we learn to establish the conditions under which our children can hopefully discover a sincere gratefulness and genuine wonder regarding the Father, Son, and Spirit.

This extends far beyond compulsory Sunday school, church attendance, or youth group. It requires that we as fathers model a relationship with God that is authentic and based in humility, surrender, and wonder. Our children need to see us working out and celebrating our salvation in a continual process of sanctification. It also means that we need to be in relationship with other spiritually minded fathers who can affirm, challenge, and support us in our journeys with Christ.

Men are struggling with what it means to father well. Coming to fathering-age now is a population of dads directly influenced by feminism, psychotherapy, and the absence of their own fathers. While there are greater expectations for men to be relationally adept, we are largely ill-equipped to meet this demand. Some of us men refuse to develop the maturity to navigate in the deep waters of our relationally centered children. Because of the postmodern father's psychological socialization, we have not acquired the ability to stay in intimate, long-term relationship. It's not that we desire cold, impersonal relationships with our children—far from it. In fact, a study by the Radcliffe Public Policy Center reported that 82 percent of men from twenty-one to thirty-nine years old deemed a family-friendly work schedule to be very important, and 71 percent said they would be willing to lose pay in order to spend more time with their children. But in this post-feminist age, many men are unclear on what a man is to be (let alone what defines a father). In the face of all this, how do you and I prepare to be dads? We don't have all the answers, but we are pretty sure it begins with becoming more of the man you were made to be. Pursue passion. Risk courageously. Fight battles. Be noble. Surrender to God. Walk in truth. Live in the light.

BEST OUTINGS

FOR OUTINGS, YOU WILL NEED:
- A stroller or front carrier or backpack—what to get depends upon what activities you most enjoy.
- Diaper bag—it's a great idea to laminate an index card on which you've written everything that needs to be packed in the diaper bag before leaving home; that way, anyone can pack the diaper bag by checking the list.
- Car seat—to transport baby safely.

TIPS FOR TAKING YOUR BABY OUT:
- In crowds, leave the baby in the infant car seat and drape a blanket over the handle. This will allow him to rest without interruption and will keep germs away. Other children love to see new babies, and you can keep them from sharing unwanted illnesses by telling them that your baby loves to have her toes touched.
- Always have a feeding plan.
- Know where there are diaper changing stations. Many shopping centers, malls, and department stores offer nursing mother rooms, so be sure to ask if one is available.
- Choose to go places where a crying baby will not be a huge disruption. If you choose a quiet, romantic restaurant to celebrate your anniversary, chances are your sweet little angel will not be angelic.

IDEAS FOR OUTINGS
- Walks
- Picnics
- Sporting events/mellow concerts (take cotton balls to put in the ears).
- Family-friendly restaurants
- Friends' houses
- Zoo
- Park
- Hiking
- Library
- Shopping
- Running errands (especially home improvement stores, pet stores, sporting goods stores—these are like field trips for young children).
- Boating/trips to the lake

> **"Do, or do not. There is no 'try.'"**
>
> —Yoda, *The Empire Strikes Back*

CHAPTER 10
What Do I Do Now?

Periodically, my (David) wife leaves me alone with all three of our children. I believe this choice once made her feel unsettled. I think she secretly feared for their safety. Strange and dangerous things sometimes happen when I'm left alone for long periods of time with the kids. I know she frets over their food intake while in my care. I tend to feed with an emphasis on convenience at the expense of dietary concerns. In my mind, there is no reason why you couldn't have peanut butter and jelly sandwiches with pretzels three meals a day if it's available and everyone enjoys it as much as they do. Food is one of the many areas of parenting where my wife responds with greater intention.

Yesterday she ventured off, and I was alone for several hours with my three little ones. I was attempting to make breakfast (a.k.a. cereal with milk and a breakfast bar). My children were playing and laughing together in the playroom that is just off our kitchen. They aren't always *just* playing and laughing together. One should always savor those moments. Just as I was pouring the milk, my four-year-old yelled out, "Dad, Witt's peanut is loose." I paused and wondered to myself what in the world she could be reporting. Continuing with my breakfast preparation, I responded by asking, "What peanuts are you talking about?" She yelled back, "He only has one peanut, Dad." Meanwhile, my other two-year-old son started chanting, "Peanut, peanut." I decided it would be a good idea to explore

....

this situation a little closer. As I was moving toward the playroom, she screamed in disbelief, "His diaper is coming off, and he is touching his peanut now. Hurry! Hurry!" Baker chanted louder, "Peanut! Peanut!"

I rounded the corner and caught a glance of my two-year-old son sitting on the floor, a look of confusion mixed with pleasure on his face. His diaper had given way from a night of urinating freely in his sleep and pulled itself apart on one side. His masculinity, also known to my daughter today as his "peanut," had wiggled right out. By this point, Baker was dancing around the room shaking a maraca yelling, "Peanut, peanut, Witt has a peanut."

CONFUSION AND PLEASURE

This morning while making breakfast, I smiled thinking about yesterday morning and the peanut extravaganza. I remember seeing my son's look of confusion and pleasure. I am committed to doing everything I know to do throughout my boys' lives to instill a sense of confidence in how they were designed. I want them to feel comfortable with being masculine and all that encompasses. I want them to feel safe in asking questions aloud about who they are and how they were created. I want them to know they were constructed to be strong and courageous, tender and compassionate. Over time, I want them to know that their presence and their words have the power to bring life and hope.

I also realize there will be moments in my sons' journeys into manhood when they will experience confusion and the feeling of being "exposed." As I have said before, there are no other places in my own life where I have felt as exposed as I do in the arena of marriage and family. I can't tell you the number of times I have asked the question, "What do I do now?" I have asked that question in great fear and confusion. I have experienced a hundred moments of feeling as if I'm sitting in the middle of a room, exposed to the world, with chanting all around me, questions circling, and people rushing in, and not having a clue what to do.

I recently wandered into a local bookstore in town that I enjoy and found seven different books in the parenting section written on the subject of what to do if your baby is crying in the middle of the night. This is a hot and controversial subject. There are many schools of thought around this issue. These books offer a range of options and opinions on how to help him/her sleep peacefully. There were a couple of books addressing what to do when your wife is crying in the middle of the night with your baby. I couldn't, however, find a book that spoke to what to do when you feel like joining your infant and wife in the act of hysteria. That is one of the reasons Stephen and I wanted to write this book. We desperately wanted to speak to the uncertainty and incompetence we experience in the journey of being fathers. Where do you go when life begins to unravel and your "peanut is loose" . . . when you feel exposed, confused, and alone?

CARDIAC EXPOSURE

Perhaps my (Stephen) most exposing moment as a parent so far came with my daughter. She was about fourteen months old. We had just moved to Seattle, Washington, in order for me to attend graduate school. While this was a great opportunity for me to expand myself and for our family to grow closer, it was also hugely disruptive. I had never lived more than fifty miles from my place of birth (and my wife had just barely beaten that). And if you have ever been to both Nashville and Seattle, you know that they are quite different places.

Nashville, my hometown, is known as Music City USA, the Buckle of the Bible Belt, and the Athens of the South. Geographically, Nashville, the heart of the Southeast, sits in a bowl of gently rolling hills. It is a medium-sized southern city with mostly traditional values and views on life. "Nashvegas" plays home to the country and Christian recording industries, the Southern Baptist Convention, the Hospital Corporation of America, and more than six universities (the most famous being Vanderbilt). In Nashville, you will find a unique blend of hard drinking music types, big-haired churchgoers, and highly educated professionals (many times this describes a single person). Seattle, known as the Emerald City, is the economic, cultural, and civic hub for the entire Pacific Northwest. Geographically, Seattle is pinched between the Olympic Mountains, the Cascade Mountains, and the Puget Sound. The largest West Coast city north of San Francisco, Seattle prides itself on being edgy, socially progressive, and culturally inclusive. It's the birthplace to grunge, Starbucks, Microsoft, and REI. Here you will meet coffee snobs, dot-com millionaires, and wannabe throwbacks.

So, there I was with my daughter, sitting on the bathroom floor a few weeks after we had moved. I had just given her a bath and was drying her off. She was this slippery ball of giggling flesh draped in a towel. I don't exactly remember what we were doing except that we were laughing and had stumbled into an intense moment of intimacy between us. She was with me, and I was with her—I was unaware of anything else besides that moment.

Then it happened in an instant. She looked up from where she was crouched on her hands and knees, her intense gaze looking straight into my eyes, and she smiled. I thought my heart might explode with joy. Immediately following the rush of joy, I was overcome by a wave of toxic shame that said, "I'm not worth this. If she really knew me, she would look away." But she didn't.

We sat there in silence together, her smiling and staring into my soul. For a moment, I hated her for what she had exposed in me. She touched me someplace deep, and she had found a hidden wound. It was more than I could bear. I looked away and broke her gaze. "Wait!" my heart screamed, but it was too late. She got the message. "You can get close to me, and we can have fun, but don't you dare love me that much." I tried to find her eyes and couldn't. She would not look back at my face for many, many months.

Room to Breathe

I don't know why God let me be so aware in that moment, but I am thankful. This transaction with my daughter was the impetus for a journey that has been rich in personal meaning, healing, and change. Before this moment, I was oblivious to the power and implications of my own story in my life. While the dignity and depravity in my life is wholly different from other men, how these events have shaped me is entirely unique.

Through my daughter's eyes, I began to learn that the best way to participate with my children and my wife was to be more and more of myself. I am discovering that the more that I know myself and my desires and live those out in my life, the more I am able to join my wife and children in the midst of their lives. Until that moment with my daughter, I treated my life more as a formula and equation than I did a story—trying to figure out the answer to the questions without ever really addressing the value of the questions in the first place. As I am learning to love my story, I am learning to love myself, my family, and my God.

Saint Basil wrote, "Memory is the cabinet of the

imagination, the treasury of reason, the registry of conscience, and, the council chamber of thought." Like mine, your life is a story, too. The more willing we are to "re-remember" the events, characters, and themes of our lives, the more we will be able to live with passion with our wives and children. Many men are living numb. They don't have an awareness of the range of emotion and desire that is available to them. We are only limited in the amount of joy we can experience by the amount of grief we refuse to face.

Engaging Your Heart

I (David) mentioned that I counsel a lot with boys. Most of the boys I counsel are between the ages of ten and eighteen. I spend a lot of my day exploring issues surrounding pre-, mid- and late-adolescence. Needless to say, I have had a number of conversations about sexual development. I particularly enjoy helping fathers in conversations with their own sons around these issues. Most fathers I encounter are as painfully uncomfortable with the "sex" topic as their sons are hearing from them on it. Much of that comes from the fact that the majority of us never had this kind of conversation with our own fathers. If we did, many times it was awkward, fast, and like something out of a textbook. Therefore, the idea of dialoguing openly around these issues seems foreign.

Years ago, I shared several conversations about sex with a father named Greg. Greg was a certified public accountant—a numbers man. His son was fourteen and had stumbled onto pornography over the Internet. Greg and I talked about the importance of coming behind this incident with an effort not to shame his son, but to acknowledge a natural curiosity based on where he is biologically and developmentally. We discussed the emotional impact on a boy who experiments with pornography, educating him effectively, and what kind of boundaries to put in place for him at this point.

Our conversation then moved in the direction of discussing how much (or how little in this case) he had talked with his son about anything of a sexual nature. Greg talked of how his father had prepared a "birds and bees" conversation for him at twelve that was informative, included diagrams, but felt a bit like a Sunday School lesson. He remembered it happening, but didn't remember it having impact. He confessed that he intended to do something different with his own son, but had let time get away from him. We agreed that a golden opportunity had presented itself to make up for some lost time.

Time passed, and we ended up having three different conversations between the two of us without Greg engaging his son. Greg's procrastination continued to open the door for us to discuss his story, his father, and his fear. I reminded him on several occasions that all his son needed from him was his presence, and the rest would unfold over time. He had the hardest time believing that there wasn't more preparation required.

On our fourth appointment, Greg came in smiling. He had a skip in his step and a look of accomplishment on his face. He announced before he had even taken a seat that the conversation had finally happened. I asked him to share with me what that time had been like for the two of them. He began speaking at length about his strategy and his words. Ten minutes into the story, I felt the need to ask, "Did you use PowerPoint in this conversation?" The conversation was sounding more like a presentation to me. Greg, the numbers man, had great difficulty not falling back on what he knew. His father's informative discussion, complete with diagrams, had been his model for his own father/son conversation.

Despite our dialogue regarding his presence being the key component, he desperately believed there was more preparation required.

Greg and I were able to laugh as he recalled details from the conversation, and he eventually wept as he spoke of feeling incompetent in his role as a father. I invited him to share his tears with his son . . . to begin the conversation by saying, "I wish my dad had been willing to talk with me this honestly about something this important." I challenged him to see this conversation as an ongoing opportunity he had to introduce his son to masculinity. I encouraged him to handle it with humor, authenticity, and to leave his laptop out of the conversation. I acknowledged the importance of being exact in his line of work, but reminded him that what parenting involved was plagued with mystery and uncertainty. I encouraged his presence and his participation through just being in the moment.

Today, Greg and I laugh about his first stabs at engaging his son around topics as sensitive as wet dreams and masturbation. His conversations have continued to look different since that time. I remind him often of what he is giving his son through his vulnerability, presence, and participation.

A Reclaimed Heart

What Greg was lacking was the knowledge and courage to live from his heart. Greg could not participate because his own father had failed to teach him the value of a man with a passion-filled heart. In order for Greg to begin to move toward his own son with wisdom, integrity, and love, he first had to acknowledge his own woundedness. What Greg had to learn was that, more than anything else, his son needed the experience of his father's heart alive to life. Greg wasn't able to do that until he faced his own painful heartache.

The human heart is what Oswald Chambers refers to as "the radical region of life." And it is in this territory that God longs most to engage and transform us. As Chambers points out:

> According to the Bible, thinking exists in the heart, and that is the region with which the Spirit of God deals. We may take it as a general rule that Jesus Christ never answers any questions that spring from a man's head, because the questions which spring from our brains are always borrowed from some book we have read, or from someone we have heard speak; but the questions that spring from our hearts, the real problems that vex us, Jesus answers those. The questions He came to deal with are those that spring from the implicit center. These problems may be difficult to state in words, but they are the problems Jesus Christ will solve.[1]

Until we are willing to drop the barriers that surround our hearts and open them to God and our family, we will miss out on the full experience of life. Jesus makes it clear: "The kingdom of heaven is near." The keys to this kingdom are a surrendered, healed, and transformed human heart.

Sometimes, we men need assistance in the work of reclaiming our hearts and living from our stories. Often this aid comes from a friend, mentor, family member, pastor, or possibly even a counselor. With our hearts transformed and passionately alive to life, we will be able to move more deeply into our children's lives and offer them the things our fathers never offered us. We often avoid these opportunities to wrestle with God in our stories and instead look for a quick fix or a proven formula for success— anything to find a solution.

1. Oswald Chambers, *Biblical Psychology: Christ-Centered Solutions for Daily Problems* (Discovery House Publishers, Grand Rapids, MI: 1995).

HABITS AND FORMULAS

Our culture is intoxicated by the promises and predictions of what we call the "Habit Movement." It has been around for quite some time now. We have half a dozen theories on why we crave mastery and twice as many books that tell us how to do it. There are habits for a successful marriage, principles for parenting, laws for leadership, and on and on. While many of these concepts are sound and effective tools for success, the most common denominator is a blueprint for mastery. It is such an attractive illusion that "if only I master these twelve effective practices, I am guaranteed success." We desperately want this to be true. We love money-back guarantees.

My (David) wife laughs at me every time I fantasize about having enough money to buy a new car every time the warranty expires, so that I'd have free mechanical service at my disposal for the rest of time. I want the guarantee that if I have a problem, it's taken care of immediately, effortlessly, and without expense. Wouldn't it be nice if all of life worked this way? And doesn't it suck that life is rigged not to work this way?

So, why do we continue to live as if it isn't? I genuinely believe that there is some warranty regarding life this side of heaven. That's why the self-help books sell in the millions. We are chasing the belief with great intensity that if I just do the right thing, I will have the right life. While this is generally true with money, it is almost never true with parenting. But that desire is as strong in me as it has ever been. I want to know there is a money-back guarantee with my children. I need to know that if I contribute a certain investment in each of my kids, it will yield expected results.

Participation vs. Activity

All of these habits center around activity. As men, we are creatures of movement. We often feel most engaged when we're doing something. We enjoy feeling productive. This is one of the reasons that the processes of pregnancy and parenting can be challenging for us. It involves a great deal of waiting. Furthermore, the participation doesn't always lend itself to activity.

Participation and activity are two different things. Sometimes participation involves activity, but not always. Often it involves waiting . . . like sitting on a hanging curve ball just long enough to jack it out of the park. It's in that space where challenge lies for us as men. As long as we're doing something, we feel productive and purposeful. The challenge is that participation is more a process of being than doing. Much of pregnancy and parenting involves waiting. Waiting on this baby to come. Waiting on joy. Waiting to connect. Waiting on God to show up. Waiting on your child to learn through natural consequences. Waiting on the hope that you believe in but don't yet see. Waiting and waiting and waiting.

Participation goes hand in hand with the experience of parenting. For us as men, stepping onto the field is a part of our participation. Participation is also the activity you are engaged in at this very moment. Reading this book, taking a class with your wife, painting a nursery, researching pediatricians, investigating schools . . . these are all vital and important experiences. We hope you are a part of every one of them. But you must understand that sometimes participation simply involves presence— presence with the belief that you bring something valuable and needed to this process.

Radney Foster has some great lyrics about joining in the process without having a clue what to really do.

You always see right through the smoke and mirrors, nothing fooled you for long.
You know there's just a man behind a curtain shifting gears.
Still making it up as I go along.
I've worn this mask before 'til I don't know who I am.
I love the cards life's dealt me, but I sure don't know how to play out my hand.

The last line really hits home with what it feels like to be a father. This song speaks to the uncertainty we experience as men in relationship, but also to the value of our presence. There is something so courageous about stepping into the question of "What do I do now?" realizing you won't always be able to answer that question with certainty or clarity. My response will involve offering my presence, remembering the value of simply showing up. Show up, step on the court, and believe you bring something valuable to the table. There's your answer.

WHAT TO DO?

What do you do now? You could do a lot. Doing something is the first and most important step. But we think there are at least four things you must do to be an exceptional father:

1. Love your wife well.
2. Have good male friends.
3. Risk your ego.
4. Learn from your kids.

Love Your Wife Well

I (Stephen) love my wife more than I could ever describe, but I rarely love her well. In my role as a father, the one area that I need to improve more than any other is as a husband. I fall way shorter than I desire in my capacity to love Heather as she deserves.

Tonight, we got into a really sad argument. The core of the conversation is the same dispute we've been having for our ten years of marriage:

- I overlook her in favor of my own passions, vocation, achievements, and vision.
- And I take advantage of her willingness to serve and care for my needs.

While the core of the dialogue is intact, the words swirling between us have grown more and more honest and accurate over the years. Defensiveness has given way to desire. Anger has melted into heartbreak. Fear has been conquered by trust. What remains constant is that I truly am a selfish jerk. Courageous, devoted, honest, lovable, and passionate, yes, but a jerk all the same.

My failure to invest fully in growing Heather's desire and beauty leaves me taking advantage of her. More often than not, I put myself first. I know this. I have known this. Heather and others tell me this. But no matter how diligently I commit to change, I can't fully escape the gravity of my own ego. My world revolves around me, and as Scripture admonishes, like a dog, I return to my own vomit.

But this gives hope for me as a father. I have learned that because Heather and I are willing to stand before God and stay in the grips of conversation, our children benefit by having a family grounded in the stability of intimacy and honesty. For all that I fail at as a husband, I have helped create a marriage safe enough for my wife to be honest with me about who I am with her. She is committed to calling me to be the man God wants me to be. In return, my children get a father who will grow in his faith—one inch at a time.

HAVE GOOD MALE FRIENDS

We believe strongly that you can gauge the extent a man lives from his heart by the depth and quality of relationships he has with other men. If you want to be a good husband and father, you need deeply authentic relationships with other men. There is something so vital about sharing life with other men. When we speak of sharing life, we are referring to relationship that involves authenticity and vulnerability. Conversation that centers on more than sports, cars, and politics. Relationship even goes well beyond the parameters of traditional Bible study. Many Christian men believe they are experiencing this kind of relationship when they join a "men's group." As valuable as it is to come together with other men and engage in study of the Word, read a book, hang out, or share prayer requests, we believe it must go beyond this. Here are some core questions to ask yourself in thinking of shaping your relationships with other men:

1. Do you have a man in your world who has seen you in some of your weakest moments?

2. Do you have a man in your life who is willing to stand in your way? To confront you? To offend you for the sake of your higher good?

3. Do you have a man in your life who has a vision for you,

who sees good in you and seeks to draw it out? Is there a man who would ask you if you are loving your wife in front of your children?

4. Is there a man to whom you can confess sexual sin? What about confessing greed, envy, or hate?

5. Is there a man in your life who reminds you to speak and to remember?

6. Do you know a man who quiets you and reminds you of the goodness of God?

Really consider if your life involves relationships of this kind. Don't fool yourself into believing you're exempt from this. No man is. Similarly, don't deceive yourself into believing that your wife can be this person for you or that it is even her responsibility. Certainly, she may do some of these things. She likely is a person who sees good in you and who reminds you of truth. She should never be the person who is solely responsible for confronting you or standing in your way. You need men to accomplish this.

Risk Your Ego

Recently, Stephen invited me to coach. The majority of my friends and family find this invitation particularly humorous, not because I've never coached the sport of soccer before, but because I've never even played a game of soccer in my life. I don't really even know the rules of the game. You may remember my description of the small, rural community where I was born and raised. We didn't have soccer as an option in the late seventies and early eighties. The game of soccer didn't come on the scene in Bedford County until I had moved away and was in graduate school. In this day and age, most high schools offer every sport imaginable. You can choose from football to water polo, from rugby to table tennis. A student I work with even plays Frisbee golf as a school sport. The only lettering sports offered at my alma mater were football, basketball, and cow tipping. It's a new day and time. This small-town boy wouldn't have known what to do with all those options. However, I believe I would have explored the sport of soccer if only I'd been given a shot at it.

You may be wondering to yourself why Stephen believed I would benefit the coaching staff. Quite frankly, I am wondering the same thing. There is one advantage to this coaching experience: my entry into the world of coaching soccer. It's the four-year-old league, and my belief is that I may know just as much as they do about the game of soccer. Their parents, on the other hand, may be a bit of a challenge. I'm planning to adopt some of the lingo and master some commands before the first practice. I want to give the illusion of being more seasoned than I am. Because let's be honest—these parents aren't interested in turning their future athletes over to a nincompoop.

Our team is the Crickets. I have a particular investment in this team because one of the Crickets is my daughter, Lily. She is joined by Stephen's daughter and ten other little female soccer warriors, who will be trained to deliver the ball to the goal at whatever cost, taking down anyone who stands in their way. We will disguise that objective as something more appropriate and sportsmanlike. Nonetheless, this will be their chief purpose and focus . . . except for when, like my daughter, they are concerned about their shin guards getting too dirty or needing to adjust their ponytails. I am loving this opportunity before me.

I just experienced a what do I do now moment this afternoon. The Crickets had their first official team soccer practice a few hours ago. We had some classic moments with our little army of four-year-old girls. At least 50 percent of the time, the girls were running toward one of the two goals. They spent about 20 percent of the remaining 50 percent of the time at least running after a ball somewhere out of bounds. For the remainder of the time, the Crickets took a lot of potty and water breaks.

My sweet daughter was much more interested in her water bottle, how well her shin guards match her practice shorts, and which mom brought the snacks. She has always been more of an observer than a participant . . . not just in the game of soccer, but in the game of life. My chief objective in having her play was just to provide an opportunity for her to participate . . . to get in the game. When I wasn't watching the bigger picture (as all good coaches should do), I would catch her out of the corner of my eye wandering in the midst of the giant huddle chasing the ball. She seemed somewhat interested and at times a bit eager, but always tentative. I attempted to nudge her in the direction of the play with words of encouragement and support. She would pick up her step from time to time and move near the ball, and then she would resume her position outside the circle watching the action.

I could feel something strong stirring in me. A part of me wanted to push her harder to move toward the play at hand. I'm certain a part of that was rooted in my objective to have her get in the game. The other part of it was likely my awareness of all the parents along the sidelines observing this sweet little blonde wandering about, and my performance issues kicked in. Just moments before sitting down to write, I became acutely aware that there's a lot of sadness stirring in me as well. I'm sad that the part of my daughter that wants to stand outside the game is my genetic contribution. The tentativeness, the hesitation, even the anxiety that she often experiences around entering into new situations can be traced right back to dear old dad. That was so much my story. I have lived much of my life fearful of getting in the game. What do I do now?

I chose this time to offer to run with her. I traveled across the field moving toward her until she caught my eye. I ran straight to her and grabbed her hand. I invited her to run with me. We would attempt to dribble the ball together. It seemed to be just what she needed. She held my hand tightly, and we headed toward the huddle. Just as we were nearing the ball, she melted. Tears started pouring down her face. She couldn't control her tears and began to weep. My heart ached. My touch had accomplished what I had intended with unexpected results. I wanted her to feel safe enough to enter into the game. Instead, my touch made her feel safe enough to fall apart. Henri Nouwen once said, "I had been received with open arms, given all the attention and affection I could ever hope for, and offered a safe and loving to place to grow spiritually as well as emotionally. Everything seemed ideal. But precisely at that time, I fell apart—as if I needed a safe place to hit bottom."

I desperately want my efforts in fathering to breed courage, hope, and joy in my children's lives. I want my efforts to be enough, and they never will be. Only the God who made each of my children, with their own design, is capable of bringing hope and joy into their lives. I believe He simply wants me to be present in their lives. And He wants me to move them toward the only One who can offer them fulfillment. My presence did provide a sense of safety for my daughter this afternoon—the safety to weep. I believe I will be called to that place again and again. It is a vulnerable space.

As practice came to a close, we said goodbye to our new teammates. We packed up our gear, we had our post-practice snack, and everyone moved toward their vehicles (mostly minivans, I would like to note here). Lily asked if we could stay and have practice just the two of us. I said, of course we can. We dribbled the ball down the field. She smiled and laughed, and I cheered every time she kicked into the goal as if it were the needed points for a World Cup victory. I was reminded that she may likely always love the slow, quiet moments of life spent one-on-one more than any other time. Afterward, we lay in the grass and talked about the time. I was making it all up as I went along. It felt unknown, and it just felt good. Tears and laughter, the whole package. I just want to live fully, love deeply, and lead in some way.

An old Spanish proverb advises, "Where there is love there is pain." This is certainly proven true in the realm of my parenting. If we, as fathers, choose to meet our children in the whoop and wailing of life, we will experience heartache. To love our children well and want good things for them means that when they hurt, we hurt, when their hearts break, ours do, too. It is hard to stay in these moments because it stokes so much of the pain and passion from our own lives.

Learn from Your Kids

Athletics have been an important part of my (Stephen) life, and I am committed to sharing this passion with my children. I have a love for all types of sport (except for the NBA: I grew up in the era of Magic, Michael, Carl, and Scotty, and today's brand of pro basketball fails to hold my attention). On Sundays in the fall, we curl up on the couch together to watch the Tennessee Titans. This spring, my four-year-old daughter and I had second-row seats for the

U. S. Women's National Soccer Team. (I wanted her to see Mia Hamm before she retired.)

At the writing of this book, I am watching the 2004 Summer Olympics with my wife and daughter. This is a big deal for her in that she gets to stay up much later than her 7:30 bedtime. Together we have enjoyed swimming, track and field, and platform diving (which she calls "water diving"). Sports for us is beginning to be a shared interest and a doorway to early conversations around passion, desire, work ethic, pain, goals, and honesty.

For instance, this morning while watching the conclusion of the women's marathon, the eventual bronze medalist, an American, was crying as she made the final turn toward the finish line. "Why is she crying?" Emma Claire asked.

How do you explain to a four-year-old the concept of twenty-six miles, years of training, and being an Olympic medalist? I was at a loss for words, but I took a stab at it, "Well, you see," I began, and then launched into this drawn-out explanation of struggle, training, dedication, competition, etc., which ended with something like, "She's done all she can do to be who she is. She won, and now it's over."

"So, she's happy *and* sad," Emma Claire replied.

"Yes, honey. She's happy and sad," I affirmed. My daughter spoke more directly to the expression of joy on that runner's face than any of my explanations. If I stop and listen to my kids with my heart, I will often discover that they have a way of revealing the simple beauty and truth of life.

Like the other day with my son Elijah. We recently bought a house, and with the first rain after we moved in, the driveway flooded. Two inches of standing water covered most of the blacktop. I thought to myself, *The first project will be to install French drains.* When the rain stopped, my family walked out to the mailbox. My wife, daughter, and I went around the driveway through the yard. Not my toddler son, Elijah. He broke right for the puddle and splashed until he was soaked head to toe. As his personality begins to more clearly emerge, I am discovering how bent toward adventure his heart is. Since he could crawl, Elijah has had an aversion to sidewalks. He has never met a mulch pile he hasn't tried to climb. If he sees a bed of rocks, he will sit down in the middle and dig, pack, and throw until he is covered with mud and grime. The more I come to know my son, the more I grow in the understanding of my own masculinity. Listing to his heart has uncovered a need for adventure and challenge in my own.

Go for It!

Being a dad is not easy. But it's not that hard, either. You were made for it. Shaped for it. Destined for this moment in your life. What do you do now? Step into the fray. Live life to the fullest. Love your wife desperately. Love your child with abandon. Throw yourself off the ledge of security and ride on the thermals of grace and wisdom that God has provided you.

Don't hold back for one second. Be a wild and dangerous lover of life. Risk for more. Dare God to show up in your story. Remember who you are and how you got here. Never forget. You will change the world by loving your children well because if you risk into the chaos of uncertainty, you will play a role in ushering in the kingdom of heaven.

> **"THERE IS A FINE LINE BETWEEN FISHING AND JUST STANDING ON THE SHORE LIKE AN IDIOT."**
>
> —STEVEN WRIGHT

CONCLUSION
Ooof

Much of my (Stephen) life is made up of "Ooof" moments. "Ooofs" are those times in life when we ignorantly do things that are so blatantly goofy that if we saw someone else do them, we would cringe with shame for them, only to grunt, "Ooof." If life were a movie, these would be the outtakes on the DVD.

The moments leading to the birth of my eldest child were full of "Ooofs." My wife, Heather, was lying in the hospital bed well into labor, and she was rigged to more medical devices than a Harvard science experiment. A belt-like gadget that monitored her contractions and the baby's heartbeat was wrapped to her belly. On her arm, she wore a cuff that automatically checked her blood pressure every few minutes. Clipped to her finger was her own heart-rate and blood-oxygen apparatus. Coming out of her left arm was an IV linked to a bag of fluids to help keep her hydrated and provide a way to administer drugs. Trailing from her back was an intravenous line that was hooked to a bag of anesthesia, which ran to a needle in her spinal column.

All of the heart and blood devices ran to an extraordinary machine that simultaneously recorded and reported the results either on a TV monitor or on a continuously fed roll of paper. A repeating beep, beep, beep, coupled with the hum of all of the equipment, made for really cool sound effects. For a kid who grew up on video games and television, the flashing lights, electronic noises, and medical drama was captivating. I was mesmerized.

Our family members, herded in the waiting room, were taking turns visiting us and wishing Heather well. I was trying my best to be a helpful husband and a gracious host. As visitors came in, I would offer them a seat, give them the latest update from the doctor, and share with them the marvels of modern medicine by giving a tutorial on the fancy-schmancy machines. "This one does _____. That one does _____. Oh, and this one, _____."

At one point, I was demonstrating the equipment to one family member with all the pride of showing off a new car loaded with all the latest bells and whistles—"Look! She's having another contraction. And it's a big one"—when from behind me, Heather grunted a response.

My shame said, "Ooof."

For me, all the flashy equipment made for the perfect distraction from the stress, fear, and excitement of the birthing process. This is only one example of how I bumbled through this delivery experience. Another was my choice of beverages. Because the hospital had rules against laboring mothers eating or drinking, I would feed her ice chips. Sweet, right? Wrong. I kindly fed Heather ice chips while I sipped on my Coke from the cafeteria downstairs.

"Ooof," again.

Or how about when Heather began to push the baby out. I stood attentively by her side waiting for what I was supposed to do. Which wasn't much. When the nurse asked if I would support Heather from behind during the next contraction, I held her back in such a way that she could neither breathe or push. I was effectively choking her.

And again, "Ooof."

Or what about when it was all over and we were resting quietly in the room with our precious new baby daughter. Heather reached into her bag and handed me a gift. It was a great watch engraved on the back with Ps. 118:23, which she told me read, "The Lord has done this, and it is marvelous in our eyes." Then it occurred to me that I didn't get her anything.

Once more, "Ooof."

To my credit, there were some moments when I was a pretty amazing husband and father, and I continue to surprise myself by being one from time to time. But, without a doubt, there are many more "Ooofs" to keep me humble. All in all, I am a pretty good father and am learning how to become better each day. I know if I can get the hang of it, you will be able to, also. And while the "Ooof" moments may never fully disappear, they sure don't affect me nearly as much.

You, too, will feel clumsy at times. There will be moments when you will not know what to do. The secret is not more knowledge, but more passion. Knowledge without passion is boring, numb, and "safe." Like Christ, God made us to be men full of passion. Passion is always dangerous, electrifying, and exhilarating. Passion, by its nature, is simultaneously alien and familiar.

Being a great dad is all about passion. Fatherhood was designed by a passionate God to be spine-tingling, unpredictable, and rewarding. Being a father is an untamed journey of the heart. If you are open to fully experiencing it, it will take you through some of the most intense joy you can ever encounter. Get ready. God has put you in a position of utmost responsibility, and you are poised for maximum achievement.

A Legacy of Life

Throughout this book, we tried to address many of the questions that stir in the hearts of new fathers. We hope that reading this book has helped you engage your life as a man and your roles as husband and father more fully. As you cast visions of ball games, first dates, graduations, and marriages, there is one more question we would like you to consider: What will be your legacy? What will be the emotional and spiritual inheritance you leave your children? What will your daughter rise up and say at your retirement dinner? What words will your son speak at your funeral? What stories will your grandchildren tell their children about their grandfather?

Any legacy we leave our child will be forged in the flames of relationship. (Being an excellent father is always about relationship.) We must endeavor to gain for ourselves and then provide our children with the necessary tools and skills needed for a full and fruitful life. (These tools are first and foremost emotional and spiritual.) Are we doing the work necessary to lay the spiritual and emotional foundation we will need to help our children shape their futures in our own lives? In other words, are you living an authentic life full of passion and married to mystery?

Are you living authentically (without secrets and hidden agendas)? Are you passionate about life? Are you willing to tolerate mystery? Are you in a process of reconciling your life to Christ? No matter what great techniques you apply and how many books you read, if you aren't willing to try to have these elements as part of your life, you will fail as a father. Without these, your legacy will be bound to what your child achieves, not who she becomes.

WILD RIDE

The water is wild. It is pouring out over the rocks, slamming against the side of our raft, and engulfing most of the photograph that I (David) am looking at in this moment. It was taken on a trip down the Ocoee River outside in Chattanooga, Tennessee, a few weeks ago. There are six men in this photograph. Each of our faces reveals something about each of our hearts. You see everything from wild enthusiasm to complete panic. Stephen put this trip together. He managed to pull five men together to take a day off from work and family to experience a day in the great outdoors. Three of us had never rafted the Ocoee before, and none of us had done the Olympic Run. The

Olympic Run is so called because it was designed for the 1996 Summer Olympic Games in Atlanta. The Ocoee River was home to the rafting events that year. What I am trying to communicate to you is that the world's finest athletes traveled from all corners of the world to raft this wild and daunting section of the river. Shortly after the Olympic games, various Ocoee outfitters began hosting trips down this portion of the river to experienced—and foolish—rafters and kayakers. Our crew would most certainly be categorized as the latter: foolish, but hungry for adventure.

Upon arrival, we were instructed in basic survival rafting 101 and educated on the nature of the river. We boarded an old bus that would drive us to the point where we would launch out and maneuver our way down the wild river. Shortly into the ride, we were introduced to our guide. His given name was Randy, but he was known on the river and to his colleagues as "Dr. Doom." Doom (as we would refer to him) was an experienced guide who had been with the outfitter for almost two decades. He was seasoned in his craft and renowned for his antics. This man's life motto was, "Always remember that if your chin's on the curb, you ain't in the gutter."

Doom was stout, his words were few, his presence was profound, and his eyes were wild. If you didn't follow his command and found yourself outside the boat, he referred to you throughout the remainder of the day as "Sally."

The photograph in question was taken moments after we had been dashed against some rocks and turned 360 degrees all in a matter of seconds. When Doom wasn't shouting, "Left forward three—NOW!" he could be heard laughing while saying, "Ladies, we're not having fun until I hear helmets slamming against each other!"

It was a wild and amazing ride. I loved it, and it terrified me. It was so similar to my experience of being a father. I love it passionately, and it scares the life out of me. I have been dashed against some serious rocks and flipped around, upside-down, and in every direction possible. And I believe I am just getting started. I am on the front side of this ride, as are you. Prepare yourself for a wild, daunting ride. Paddle forward, scream out loud, and understand that you're going to get banged around. Regardless of how much instruction you have on the front end, you may get flipped out of the boat. You may end up on your back, laid out on some rock, clueless as to what to do next. This ride is designed to disrupt you, immerse you, terrify you, excite you, and deepen you.

The photograph I am looking at is one of five photographs taken that day by photographers on the side of the river. My expression is very different in each one. In some of the pictures, I am laughing—laughing from the wildness of it all, laughing from pure exhaustion. In one of the pictures, I am staring at a major drop we are approaching. I look terrified. In another, I look content, the kind of contentment one experiences when life comes together. Circumstances came together that amazing day in September. It was the combination of great fellowship, perfect weather, and adventure, and we ended the day with a hearty meal. Good food always brings me contentment. The combination of good food and good friends is about as close to perfection as it gets for me.

Many days I can be found laughing—laughing at the realities that come with parenting my three children. Some days I look terrified—terrified by the idea of loving my wife when we are at odds with one another. At certain times, I am content. I can embrace the fullness of what I have been given—my family, my work, my friends. Other days, I live as if I have none of it. The objective for me has become living with the knowledge that all of my life is not intended to come together.

As my good friend Al says, "Life is broken." It is futile for us to live in anticipation of life always coming together. It will come together as it did on that day in September on the water. It will again. And then the next day, it will be disrupted. It may even fall apart. The hope is to live fully in the moments of laughter and contentment—and to also be present in the moments of fear and disappointment. We need to remember that every part of it has purpose and meaning. We need to live as if we really believe the greater purpose for us is transformation—to believe that sanctification takes priority over enjoyment.

DIVINE DIVIDENDS

Transformation is often painful and enraging. For me (Stephen), the greatest and most glorious discontentment I've ever known has come through the love of my children. For instance, I work way too much. It feels that I am often leaving to go somewhere, meet with clients, travel on business, or work at a seminar. When I leave, my kids sometimes hang on the car door through my window coaxing me to stay "just two more minutes." One of the greatest gifts my children give me is the sorrow and anger I feel when I leave. Most days, I can't make it down the street without a lump in my throat, or tears in my eyes, or anger in my fists. It's a daily reminder of the deep love I have for them. It is also a fuel for some significant changes I am making in my life.

But what floors me the most is that my kids shriek "Daddy" when I come home, running to tackle me at the door. They wrap themselves around my knees and waist before I can even put down my things. Often for me, this grace is too much to stand. I don't deserve this. I know my heart. I know my secret thoughts. I know how selfish I really am about my time and desires. I suspect they do, too, but they love me anyway. Their ability to love me in spite of who I am is hard to bear. It changes me (if I let it), and it can change them, too.

Every encounter you have with your child is an investment

in his future: his marriage, his children, his career, his calling. How will you help your child prepare for the unpredictable ride of life? As we have tried to pattern in this book, you will need to get your child ready to ask the heart questions that everyone must face in order to live fully. Answering them is much less important. Asking them is the great work.

Because you have read this book, you are well down the road to being an exceptional father. Not because this book is all that remarkable, but because you have exercised a willingness to pursue your own heart on behalf of your child. Congratulations! You are on your way.

You may have identified with some or all of the questions addressed in this book—these are the deeper questions of the soul. At the very least, we hope that we have helped to stir questions within you. We hope you have ventured to ask them aloud and share them with your wife, other men, and God.

THE RIGHT MAN FOR THE JOB

After reading this book, we hope you are more involved in your own story and are better engaged with your heart. If you have any doubt about yourself as a father, a husband, or a man, you must know: You are needed. You have more strength than you probably know. Your heart is capable of more love than you could imagine. You can do this.

Before the beginning of time, you were appointed to be your child's father. God has chosen you for this. He has elected you for greatness. You may or may not feel ready. You may or may not have chosen this for yourself. You may or may not know what you've gotten into. That's okay. God knows. We were all created for one reason: "to glorify God and enjoy Him forever." The only way we can do this is to live fully. That's what God is after—you fully alive, free, and exploding with passion, presence, and purpose. He is dedicated to uncovering the remarkable man you are inside. And He is willing to use whatever means necessary to do it—especially fatherhood.

We want to hear from you. We all have stories to tell and share with other dads. If you have connected with this book in any way, we want to hear your story. We love hearing from dads and learning from you guys about what fathering has been for you. What has been helpful? What has worked? How have you succeeded? How have you failed? Where have you seen God? Where has He seemed absent? What funny things have happened to you and your wife in this process or becoming parents?

It would be great to hear from you, and we would love to know your questions, comments, and stories. They can be submitted online at *www.becomingadad.net.*

God bless you,
Stephen & David

EPILOGUE

I've had very few moments occur within the flow of living where I've actually recognized an event as being life-changing while it was happening. Most often my experience has been that the most significant moments come camouflaged in the familiar, cloaked in the mundane. For instance, one afternoon a decade ago at a college cafe, I unceremoniously met the friend of a friend who turned out to be my future wife. Or there was the time a work assignment set in motion a reaction that led me to quit my job, sell my house, move my family across the country, and change professions.

Yes, it's been seldom that I've perceived a particular event as in fact changing the direction of my entire story. When these big, recognizable moments have happened, usually they were scarred with tragedy. Like when my parents told my sister and I they were getting a divorce, or when Heather called to tell me that one of my oldest friends had tragically been killed. It's been rare that these grand experiences were marked with delight. That's why Monday was so disruptive—not because of its tragedy, but rather because of its rampant joy.

As I mentioned in the book, recently Heather became pregnant for the third time. On Monday, we went to the doctor for her midterm ultrasound. This was her first sonogram of the pregnancy. She is nineteen weeks along, and we were anxious to finally see an image of the new life growing in her womb. Seeing that more than likely this is our last pregnancy, we decided to bring our children: our four-year-old daughter and two-year-old son.

With our first two children, the ultrasound was the event for me where the reality of pregnancy and fatherhood really settled in. Knowing that, I've been looking forward to this day for weeks. Life has been busy lately, and I was ready to have this pregnancy take more prominence in my daily conscious.

The technician squirted jelly over Heather's belly, turned the monitor toward us, and moved the sound-wave apparatus across Heather's abdomen. "Is this your first ultrasound this pregnancy?" the tech asked.

Heather glanced at me curiously, "Yes," she responded.

"Well . . . there are two in there," the tech said flatly.

"Twins?" we asked in disbelief.

"Yes. Twins," the tech said.

If I was waiting for reality to settle in, it fell on us like a piano. CLANG!

I reached out, gently rested my hand on Heather's forehead, and stroked her hair. My knees filled with Jell-O©, and my stomach was flipping. The blood drained from my brain, and my lips felt cold. Turning toward my daughter, I picked her up and put her in the chair with her brother. "Emma Claire, you have to move. I need to sit down."

The tech went ahead with scanning and measuring the babies. She began with baby A pointing out its femur, stomach, kidneys, head, face, and brain. Measuring everything twice. She then moved on to baby B and did the same.

By now our daughter had caught on. "Two babies!" Emma Claire exclaimed. "Are there more in there?"

I hope not, I thought to myself.

"No, just two," the tech replied.

Emma Claire climbed down from the chair and stood right next to Heather's face. "Emma Claire," Heather said in almost a whisper, "we're having twins—two babies, not just one." In hindsight this clarification was probably more for Heather and myself than it was for Emma Claire.

Emma Claire responded excitedly, "Two and two make four."

"Yes, honey, two and two do make four." Heather confirmed. We were no longer doing addition—we were now into multiplication.

Needless to say, we're very excited and very overwhelmed to be expecting twin boys in late March. I'm learning that multiple pregnancies can be really difficult on both the mother and babies. I guess God knows what He's doing—I just wish I did. Whatever He's got planned, it's obviously not the same as me. But isn't that the point? He keeps showing me again and again that whatever good I can plan for my life, He has so much more in mind.

With twins, I'd better get comfortable with this feeling of free falling. Who wants the rug under their feet anyway? How boring is that?

Lest I forget why I desired to write this book, God is teaching me all over again. Yet again, I'm learning to be a better father as I let myself be fathered by the one true Father.

Thanksgiving comes at the right time this year. I have so much for which to be thankful. The least of which is that on Monday, I was reminded how big God is and how small of a box I try and cram Him. I'm thankful for a God who is willing to blow my boxes apart.

God continues to deconstruct my perceptions, expand my expectations, and wipe out my rationalizations. In His doing so, I'm starting to see that my story is a just thread in the fabric of God's larger narrative, and His is an epic adventure that reaches back before time and stretches out into eternity. God is redeeming the world, one human heart at a time, and I am a part of that. As a father, I get to join Him, dare I say, help Him. What a story!

When will I learn that I can't out dream God? He is surely the God of more than enough.

Glory be to God!
Stephen James, November 2004